MW01503534

❖

"I always think everything is going to last forever, but nothing ever does. In fact nothing exists longer than an instant except the thing that we hold in memory."

—SAM SAVAGE, *Firmin*

❖

"Our history reminding, round all of us entwining; for reality is but a second, maybe two. A heartbeat, a breath, then through—our history reminding.

One cord binding, we realize in the finding; for reality is but a second, maybe two. Shared memory is the glue—one cord binding.

In the past residing, we reflect on ever sighing; for reality is but a second, maybe two. Everything, everyone we ever knew—in the past residing."

—YOUR EDITOR

❖

Introduction

September, 2019

If I were to stand on the edge of the Grand Canyon and yell at the top of my voice...seconds before dying instantly and suddenly...my voice would live beyond me, ever so briefly, as my voice echos off a few canyon walls before growing still.

Yet, if I were to write a story or letter that struck someone's fancy, my letter and my "written voice" will echo for many generations. The old family stories and letters we treasure today exist as written reverberations of our loved ones' voices.

And I love those old stories and letters. Maybe that makes me nostalgic, which I often am, but I also believe we can learn and laugh from the stories of our family members, who now exist only in our memories.

Rather than rummage around in boxes looking for specific stories, how much more convenient to find them in one place! Thus, the impetus for this collection.

Written memoirs, essays, letters, in short anything we put our soul into, reflects us as individuals. The reader can quickly pick out the threads of personality woven through the fabric of the text. It is no exaggeration to say we hear the author's voice, resounding as we read. My sincere wish, for you the reader, is that you hear the multitude of voices and personalities enclosed in these pages. Ancestors who are gone, some over one hundred years, still speaking to us.

This anthology exists in a rough chronological order. "Rough" being the keyword, as many individual accounts overlap since some of these written memories span a lifetime.

It does one well to remember that many of these memories were written with a pencil on a pad of paper or a dip pen with sepia ink. Stream of consciousness guided the pen. Today we enjoy the benefit of computers. We can group similar paragraphs together, and make changes in grammar or spelling effortlessly. The finished product makes us sound more organized and literate than we actually are.

As you will notice, I have left much of the original grammar and spelling mistakes. Some corrections or changes were necessary, especially paragraph breaks, but these were done only after considerable thought in how to accomplish the needs of this book, balanced with the uniqueness of each author. Our quirks in communication make us recognizable; personality exists even in our mistakes. In addition, each specific era of the English language has its own flavor. And there are a wonderful combination of flavors in the following pages.

Navigating family relationships can be tricky and our mind sometimes struggles to draw connections. To that end I have added relationship diagrams, which can be found at the back of this manuscript. Pared down and condensed these diagrams include only the voices found in the following chapters and enough other family to make sense. Complete sibling groups are lacking, for example. While regrettable, this was necessary to fit each diagram into the confines of a page. A solid line oval surrounding a face indicates this person is one of our voices. Dotted line ovals denote people who are not voices, but necessary additions to complete the diagram.

To economize on hyphens and "great's", I will, for the most part, refer to grandparents as Grandpa or Grandma, instead of the exact relationship, which might be great-great-great or some variation thereof. The exact relationship can be seen in the diagrams.

The reader will undoubtedly notice this anthology is also a history of Woodland, the tiny community located about 12 miles north of Kamiah, Idaho. Woodland exists, in a sense, like a castle in the sky surrounded on three sides by the steep canyon walls of the Clearwater River and Lolo Creek (and the confluence of the two). 2,000 feet of elevation exists between the bench that is Woodland and the canyon floors below. Kamiah and Pardee, the two main jumping off points for travel to Woodland during this era, are situated along the Clearwater River. When the railroad reached Pardee around 1900, a road was quickly scratched into the canyon wall, switchbacking up those 2,000 feet to Woodland above.   You will read of the difficulty involved in traveling to Woodland in that pre-road era, but words scarcely convey the reality.

My maternal grandmother and grandfather were both raised in Woodland from pioneer families and likewise, my paternal grandparents. My mother and father were raised a mile apart and knew each other from their childhoods.   Nearly all of the following stories involve Woodland, from the humble beginnings of the community to the lives lived therein.

The stories of these early pioneers and their children, as they struggled to live in a society more impoverished and bereft of money than I have experienced, should inspire all of us...and challenge our norms of what is really important.

❖

CHAPTER ONE
Della Haskins (1889-1967)

Della Celeste Haskins, 1913

[Editor's notes: Before Grandpa Haskins came to Idaho from Kansas, he and his family moved from Iowa to the Nebraska-Kansas line. Both moves were accomplished by covered wagon, the ubiquitous coach or "travel trailer" of the day. Della Haskins penned this account in 1927. The "grandfather Haskins" she refers to is John Haskins, my great-great-

great-grandfather, father of Sarah Haskins, who as you will shortly read, came with her husband and four little girls by wagon train to Idaho.

This short account illustrates some of the difficulties of life in those pioneer days in Kansas and Nebraska. We are so blessed in this day and age and know not the concept of just surviving...of wondering where the next meal might come from.

John was a farmer and preacher of the United Brethren faith. Some say that his wife Nancy was also a preacher.

The picture of Della is from her wedding day. In this uncropped picture, Della is missing her left arm below her elbow. How she suffered this loss is unknown.]

John & Nancy Haskins at their sod home near Guide Rock, Nebraska.

Della's Memories

In the spring of 1871, fifty six years ago, grandfather Haskins with his wife and five children, in company with Mr. Hardy's, Mr. Connely's, Sam Kelsay's and Bert Sloan came from Iowa and all camped for a time on Star Creek on what is now the Frank Kaufmann farm. Grandfather homesteaded a quarter section on Star Creek and on a part of the old homestead, one of the girls, Mrs Carey George, still resides. *[When Della was two years of age, in 1892, her mother, Amy Ellen "George" Haskins died. Della went to live with her aunt and uncle, Carey George and Laura Haskins. You will see Della's name mentioned in Laura's chapter upcoming.]* They brought their cow with them and would strain both nights and mornings milk in a churn in one corner of the wagon. By night the milk would be sour and the jar of the wagon would have churned a little pat of butter on top of it.

Indians were still roaming the plains and the children were very much afraid of them. In the fall when the supply of bread stuff ran short the eldest boy was sent to Beatrice for more. He didn't return as soon as expected and one night when there was nothing for supper but roasting ears my Aunt says she cried and wouldn't eat any supper fearing the Indians had killed her brother and they would all starve to death.

There were still some buffalo, elk, antelope and deer in the country. As grandfather was a good hunter they usually had meat. They mixed corn meal and sorghum molasses together and browned it in the oven and of this they made "coffee". Later when they had rye they browned it and used it for coffee. They usually had white flour or bran biscuits for breakfast on Sunday mornings, but the rest of time it was corn bread, then more corn bread. The mothers those days had no such problem as we do trying to send school lunches that are both nourishing and appetizing. They took corn bread and sorghum with no thot of whether it contained the right number of calories. They made "plum leather" by cooking wild plums and pressing them threw a colander then spread out in sheets to dry. Pumpkins were cut up in strips and dried, then soaked over night before cooking.

The first school house was on the Kaufman farm, made partly of logs and part dug out. E. Peters was the first teacher and he received $25 a month and boarded himself. While Dan Waganer, a brother of Rev. N.B., was teaching school, my aunt say she fed and watered his hogs for 5¢ a day and that she was coining money. She never had a piece of money of her own until she was twelve years old and that was a 3 cent piece.

The children sometimes had strange pets, once they had a pet antelope that would follow them about like a dog, then there were two little elks but grandfather sold them, another time it was a buffalo calf, but he wasn't such a gentle playfellow, for once when grandmother went to feed it, it bunted her in the mouth knocking some teeth loose. I never learned what became of it. There were a number of rattle snakes here then and once my father was bitten on the heel, grandfather slashed the wound with his knife to let it bleed freely but father went to the house crying and thinking he would surely die. The brand of whiskey made in those days was good for snake bite so it was probably kept on hand.

My father in law the late J.J. Arrants came with his family in the spring of 76, he drove a yoke of cows with a pony in the lead arriving with only 35¢ in his pocket. He spent that for tobacco and got J.B. Toland to go his security to buy a spade with which to make his dug out. He first located on what is now known as the Arrants home place, but let his father in law, Joseph Miller have it and homesteaded an eighty that is now owned by F.M. Clark. This was shortly after grasshopper year and while times were still hard, there was some work to be had. Father got a job on Dr. Smith's sheep ranch at 50¢ a day and mother and the children held the fort at home. They got a little patch of sod broken up and mother chopped holes in it with the ax while one of the boys dropped in the corn pressing the earth over it with his foot. Thus they raised their first corn. Once when there was only one gallon of corn meal in the house and they didn't know where the next was coming from, they gave half of it to neighbor Toland's who had none at all.

I'd like to tell how the young folks used to walk several miles to church and what an awful crush some of those pioneer girls had on some of the boys, but perhaps I'd better not. But as I heard a pioneer remark recently "Those were good old days."

[In 1899 at the age of 10, Della and her brother John accompanied their uncle Carey George in guiding another family on a wagon trip to Idaho. What should have been a grand adventure, however, became an exercise in misery as Della and John suffered from measles on the trip.

As a married woman with a family, Della returned to Idaho and lived in Woodland around 1920. On March 2, 1922, her daughter Nita died

Nita Leone Arrants; with brothers Dean (above) and Dale

from injuries incurred in a sledding accident. Nita enjoyed her fourth birthday the day before the accident. Sliding with her friend Pearl Hodson (sister of Ray Hodson, chapter 14), Nita careened down an embankment and struck a picket fence. The newspaper account relates, "She got up and walked about a quarter of a mile to her home, where she was taken violently ill and remained in that condition until death came to her relief at 6:45 yesterday morning. The accident happened at 3:30 in the afternoon." Little Nita Leone Arrants is buried in the Woodland Cemetery. Her obituary stated, "She was a little sunbeam and was loved by all who knew her...A gentle voice said come, and Angels from the other side; welcomed our darling home."

Shortly thereafter, Della and the family returned to Nebraska. In December of 1926, Della and her husband Ernest welcomed another little girl in the family, Leila Faith Arrants. In 1930, in another sad month of March, they lost yet another sweet little girl as Leila became sick and passed away. Leila's obituary reads in part, "Little Faith was ill only a few days but in spite of all that love and skill could do, she slipped quietly away. Just a gleam of sunshine given to brighten our pathway for a little while."]

❖

CHAPTER TWO
Ora George (1886-1967)

Ora Ellen George, circa 1904

[Ora was John Haskins' granddaughter. John's daughter Sarah, and her husband, Austin George, came to Woodland in 1896 with their 4 daughters in tow. Ora was 9 years old and may have kept a diary of the trip.

No doubt, Grandma Ora transcribed this account from that diary or some notes that still exist of her father's. Written in pencil on older brownish lined paper, it reads almost like a list and less of a narrative. She definitely had a personality leaning toward an obsession with numbers!

One of the Ratcliff girls mentioned in this account also kept a diary during the trip. That account is more robust and will follow shortly.

I remember Great Grandma Ora well. The mother of Grandpa Harold Bacon, yet so different in personality. Grandpa Bacon was a "live wire", full of funny stories, smart cracks, mischievous to the core. Ora was a thin, quiet woman. Even at my young age, I felt she was too thin. As a child, she suffered from seizures. (Which makes me wonder, nature versus nurture, were the convulsions formative to her shy introverted makeup?)

When we visited, Grandma Rachel would inevitably persuade us to use the large wooden crank telephone hanging on the wall to call Grandma Ora. Incidentally, Ora was the first switchboard operator when Woodland jumped into the "modern age" of telephones.

Upon hearing our voices, Grandma Ora would cajole us into walking the stone's throw to visit. She made sure we all had hard candy and watched with a smile as we walked around in fascination at all the stuff packed into that big farmhouse; the house constructed by her mother Sarah after Austin's death. My favorite room was the old library upstairs. Complete with a vintage reclining daybed couch (which I now have in my library) and piled with old dusty, musty books and boxes of magazines, I could have spent days in that room. Grandma Ora was somewhat of a hoarder, with stuff stacked everywhere. She existed in a generation that had lived through difficult times and knew almost everything might be valuable in the future.

Grandma Ora died on September 21, 1967. Her funeral was the first for my siblings and I. Coincidentally, we attended our first funeral and first wedding the same weekend. The wedding was that of Aunt Sharon and Uncle Gene.]

Ora's Memories

L.E. Ratcliffs and us had our sale on the 15th. day of March 1895 and we left North Branch Kansas on April 25, 1895 starting for Idaho. In our train there was 3 men 2 women and 9 girls. Not a boy in the crowd. We had 3 covered wagons and a covered hack. Papa drove a span of mules to his wagon and Matt drove a team to the hack, and we had 1 saddle horse.

There were 5 of the Ratcliff girls and 4 of us George girls. Mabel was 11 and I 9 and Estella 5 and Lydia was 1 1/2 years old. We girls wore dresses made out of heavy moleskin and we wore red hankies tied on our heads.

[While the George girls wore red hankies on their heads, the Ratcliff girls wore blue hankies on theirs. Thus the parents had less difficulty knowing whose child was whose.]

We had a sheet iron stove and we would set the bread sponge in the morning before we left camp and at noon while we got dinner we baked the bread. You never saw bakers bread in thoes days. Left Red Cloud Nebr. April 25, 1895. Bought 2 bales of hay 90 cts. Kearney, April 29. Had horses shod, $4.00. Lexington, May 1. Bought 2 bales of hay 80c.

Gothen Berg, May 3. Bought butter 1 pound 25c. Crossed river at North Plat. May 6, Syrup 60c. At Oglealla May 8. 1 pound of butter 20¢. Big Springs May 9. 1 sack of flower 90¢. Then to Chaphle, bought 1 pound of butter 10¢. At Lodge Pole May 11. Bought wooden sugar bucket for 15¢. Still using same bucket 48 years after. *[My mother, Lorene, currently has this little wooden bucket. 125 years old and still looks new.]*

At Sidney May 13. Bought bale of hay 40¢. In Kimbel on the 14. Got pound of butter 25¢ and on into Pine Bluffs. In to Cheyenne Wyo, May 16. Got potatoes 30¢.

On May 17, was the first nite in Mts. and a man stampeded our horses but he helped to get them all back to camp again.

Then to Laramie City the 20th. Got onions 20¢. Uncle Henry killed a fat badger, couldn't eat it. There we came down off of a Mts that the road was steep and all rock. At Saratoga the 26. Got oats $7.75. Rawlins May 27. Wheat $3.90. An Irish woman told Elwood the wrong road and we was on the wrong road for 3 days where we should have made it in a day.

On May 27, crossed Green river and paid $1.50 per team for ferry. In Lewiston on June 7. Bought tea 30¢. At Pacific springs the 8. In Coke Ville on June 15. Apples 25¢. Came down an awful steep hill before we got to Cokeville and we tied trees on the back of all the wagons coming down the hill and Mama and all 9 of us girls walked down <u>ahead</u> of the teams. Before we got to Coke Ville Pappa killed a fine Antelope. We still have the horn's. *[My brother Jim currently has those horns. As children visiting the grandparents, the scruffy old antelope horns hanging on the wall looked differently when we first heard this story.]*

On the 16th of June in Idaho it snowed on us all day long. In Montpiler on the 17th. Got stockings 25¢. At Soda Springs the 19th. Shoeing Mules $2.75 and Mama sat in the wagon there and pieced quilt blocks while they shod the mules. Made Blackfoot on the 23rd. Got potatoes 20¢. Then thru desert and bought water at 25¢ a bucket for each horse. Just one day crossing the desert. Was there the 24th and we was till after dark geting off of it.

Then we got to Bellevue on the 29th. Got bacon 50¢. Then on the 4th of July we was South of Boise and Mama drove the team and Papa walked and shot Jack rabbits till he was tired.

On the 5th we came thru Boise and then on to Payette the 7th. And then we was at Weiser the 8th, and crossed Snake River there on the ferry for 25¢ a team and went on to Huntington into Oregon then up the river to La Grand. And up on top of the Blue Mts it sounded so awful hollow. And there was whare we had to pay toll bridge. And Lydia was so sick that day but was lots better the next day.

Then we came to Walla Walla Wash. and on to Dayton and then to Colfax and we landed in Palouse Wash. July the 23rd 1895. We staid in Palouse that winter and Mabel and I went to school their.

Then in March of 1896 Papa came to the Indian Reservation north of Kamiah, Idaho and filed a home stead on a 160 acres and built a log cabin on it. Then came back to Palouse after the family and we all landed here on this place on the 27 day of June 1896. And there has only been 2 nights since that time but what some of the family has been on this place, and that was in July of 1924. And this is 1943.

The first summer we dident have a floor in the house and Mama killed a ratlesnake in the house. That first winter in here they had a subscription school and each scholar paid 25¢ a month and there was just 11 scholars. Mabel and I both went.

The second summer the men all went in together and build a log school house, that was in 1897, and Papa gave them an acre of ground to build it on. The first year we had S. School and spelling school around at the homes. In July, 1898 we got the post office. And Papa named it Woodland. In 1899 they got an acre of ground for the cemetery.

In 1901 Lydia passed away the 15 of October. She was 8 years and 15 days. In 1903 there was 30 scholars going to the school in the log school house. Harley and I was each 16 and Estella was 12.

Mabel was married to Frank Finney March 16, 1902 in Kamiah, Ida. To this union was born 7 children, 4 girls and 3 boys, Florence, George, Minnie, Floyd, Avaril, Frances and Everett.

The railroad was built on up the river from Lewiston around 1900, Papa passed away the 29 of April 1908. He was 45 years and 5 months. *[Ora said almost everyone living on the hill had smallpox that spring. Exactly how many perished is unknown. Picture on following page: Log Woodland School in 1903. In the picture are Ratcliff girls, Estella George, Sanders kids, etc. all of which are mentioned in this manuscript. Subsequent picture is the wood-framed Woodland School seen upon completion and dedication in 1904. Notice the nice wooden sidewalk in front.]*

In 1910 Mama built a 9 room frame house on the place. In 1911 Harley, Estella, Fred and I were married in Lewiston on the 21 of Dec. 1911. Harley, Fred and I were 25 and Estella was 21. To Harley and Estella were born 7 children. 4 girls and 3 boys. Ray, Pearl, June, Keith, Faye and the twins, a boy and a girl. Fred and I had the one child, Harold. Mabel passed away the 28 of July, 1935. She was 51 years, 8 months and 15 days.

They have a nice church and parsonage on an acre of ground North of the cemetery. The Friends church was built there in about 1941. We saw the first plane that flew over the hill and the first car that came on the hill. There has been 6 saw mills set at different places here at Woodland. And different planers and there was a fruit dryer and there was lots of cheese made on the hill for local trade and a man made lots of butter to sell. And there was cookhouses for the mills and threshing crews. And we used to have big school fairs and a nice display of farm products, in afternoon there was a parade, led by the Woodland band of twelve pieces. Mrs. T. Campbell got first and second on best varieties of 32 kinds of fruit. *[Mr. and Mrs. Tom Campbell were neighbors to the Johnson ranch. They owned the farm now owned by Rick Simler.]* That is all has been, Nothing like that now.

There has 19 houses burned here on the hill since the first house was built.

Mama and Papa was married in Nebr. the 13 of Dec. 1882. And Mama will be 79 the 23th of this coming Nove. 1943. She was born in Iowa in 1864.

There are 16 vacant houses here and 19 that have burned down and quite a few that have been torn down. We had a big fireplace built in our log house. We traveled 25 miles a day.

The big frame school house was built in 1904 and the wing was built on to that in 1910.

I went from the first night on Jan, 1943 until the 30 of May 1944 with the lamp burning in my room every night. Just 17 moths it burned.

❖

CHAPTER THREE
Edna Ratcliff (1883-1970)

Edna Luella Ratcliff

[Edna became part of our extended family when her Uncle Harley married Estella George, Ora's sister.   Harley and Estella's son Ray Hodson, was my Grandpa Bacon's first cousin, blood-brother and best friend (that would be BBBF).

While Ora's account of the trip is rather spartan, Edna's account gives a much more complete picture of the emigration to Idaho.

Uncle Henry Haskins, member of the George-Ratcliff expedition
Girls, left to right; Ora George, Myrtle Kenworthy, Mable George, Olive Kenworthy

Like Ora, Edna's account was written later using her diary as source material. I have abbreviated her account slightly as she began her document with some general Idaho history not germane to this manuscript. Edna's account is organized, thoughtful and comprehensive. I remain just one of the many who have read and enjoyed the depth of this account. I wish I could buy her dinner, thank her and ply her with a multitude of questions.

I have read Ora and Edna's accounts several times during my life and each time I found myself reaching for an atlas. For your convenience, I created and added maps to bring further clarity to the adventure of the Georges and Ratcliffs. The maps utilize data from George Cram's state maps published in 1901. No roads are shown, as these were rare on maps of the period. Dark lines represent railroad routes and these were followed and crossed much of the journey. The group spent the majority of their travel on the Oregon and Morman trails. One notable exception is seen after Fort Hall in Southern Idaho where the group leaves the Oregon Trail taking what was then called Goodale's Cutoff. This route threads between the mountains and lava flats north of the Southern Idaho desert before rejoining the Oregon Trail around Boise.]

Edna's Memories

Introduction

Lapwai Reservation, the home of the Nezperce Indians, was opened by the government to white settlers, November 8, 1895.

The destination of the Kansas farmers and their families was this reservation where they eventually were to secure homesteads and form a community of their own. During a period of ten years, a number of these folk had left Kansas for the West. Some had traveled by team while others went by train.

Two of these farmers, with their families, the Thomas Elwood Ratcliff family, of which I was a member, and the Austin S. George family and Henry Haskins, started by team and covered wagon to Palouse, Washington on April 24, 1895. Since my father was in poor health, his physician advised him to travel out west by team.

We had disposed of our homes and sold our other possessions at auction at Austin's home on March 15, 1895.

Our caravan consisted of three covered wagons, a covered hack, a saddle horse, Old Seal, our shepherd dog, Spud, and Austin's yellow dog, Curley.

My father drove a team of horses, Lorn and Eagle, to his wagon, while my mother drove a team of horses, Barney and Dora, to the hack.

Austin drove a span of mules, Dick and Daisey, to his wagon, while Henry drove a team of gray horses, Fannie and Loren, to his wagon.

There were seven members of our family: father; our mother,

Martha Adella; myself, (Edna L.) then twelve years of age; Dosha H., age ten; Alma A., age eight; Orpah E., age five; and Olive A., age two.

The Austin S. George consisted of six members: Austin; Jeanette (Nettie), his wife; Mabel, age eleven; Ora, age nine; Estella, age five; and Lydia, eighteen months of age. Henry Haskins was Nettie's uncle.

We pitched our tents, and cooked our meals on sheet iron stoves with ovens, when we camped. We often mixed our sponge bread at morning and did the baking when cooking our noon day meal. We purchased large wooden boxes of soda crackers for $1.25 each, which often solved our bread problem. Tree branches, sage brush, splinters of wood from fence posts, that we could find on the wayside, as well as dried cow-chips were used for fuel for our stoves. As the nights were often cold, we sometimes found it difficult to keep warm.

Feed boxes for our teams were fastened to the sides and back of our wagons. We purchased hay and grain when possible, but often hobbled our teams and turned them out to graze. Our table was fastened to the back of the hack with hinges. After meals, this was raised and fastened securely.

Our mileage per day was about twenty-five miles. We seldom traveled on Sundays. Many pretty rocks were gathered for souvenirs, and flowers were pressed and sent back to friends in Kansas.

Diary

On Wednesday, April 24, 1895, we bade our friends "goodbye", left our homes and started on our journey out West. Our first destination was to be at the home of Columbus Ballard, a former Northbranch farmer, who then resided in Palouse, Washington.

APRIL 25   Our family went to the Abner Hiatt home near Esban, Kansas, our first night out. (Minnie, Abner's wife, was our cousin.) We left a part of our load to be shipped to us later on as we found the load was too heavy for our teams over rough roads.

Austin and Henry spent their first night at the Isaac C. George home (Austin's father). We met them the following morning at what was known as the Stone Church, not far distant. After traveling on for a distance of about two miles, Austin discovered that he had left his gun behind. He also found that their wagons were too heavily loaded. He went back for his gun and returned a part of their belongings to be shipped to them at a later date. After dinner, we crossed the Kansas line into Nebraska and came to a town by the name of Red Cloud and camped for the night. Orpah wondered if "Washington could be in that town".

The following morning, APRIL 26, we passed through the small town of Blayden. After traveling a distance of twenty-eight miles, we camped for the night. Our first visitors came that evening, a family by the name of Sweltzer. Their little daughter, Minnie, entertained us by singing, "Sing a Song of Sixpence".

APRIL 27 After traveling a distance of thirty miles, we came to the town of Minden. At night, our camp was three miles north of this burg.

APRIL 28 This was Sunday. A severe dust-storm came our way. Some folks visited our camp that evening.

APRIL 29 We drove twenty miles and came to the Oregon Trail at Kearney, located on the Platte River. We saw old Fort Kearney. Our teams were shod that day.

The decision was made to cross the Platte in search of better roads. When about half the distance across the narrow bridge which was one mile in length, we met a team and wagon. As the bridge had so few places that the teams could pass, it was necessary to carry their wagon around our caravan in parts. The horses were then led around us. The wind was blowing and made this a difficult task. When approaching this bridge, our dog, Spud, went below to the river for a drink of water. When he saw that we had gone on across the bridge, he began swimming in an effort to catch up with us. In some places the water was shallow and sandy;

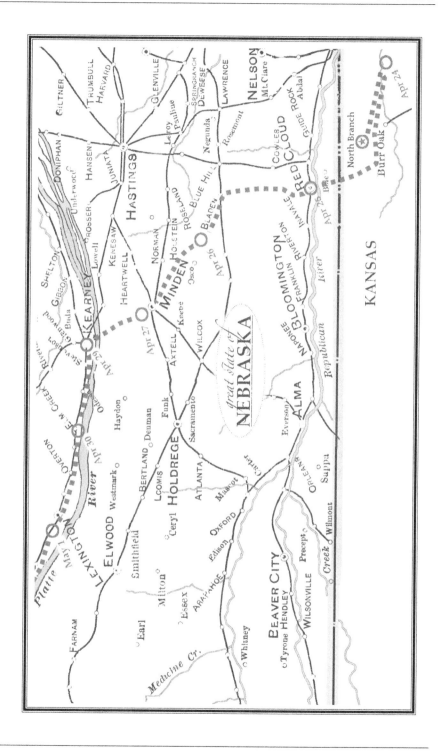

in others it was quite deep and swift. The dog barked and whined and the children cried. All were happy when the river had been crossed in safety. The water from this river was used for irrigation. We drove on for about four miles and camped. Enough rain fell to settle the dust.

APRIL 30   Some rain fell during the morning hours. In the afternoon, a heavy rain storm came our way. We went through Elm Creek Village.

MAY 1   We passed through Plum Creek town (Lexington). The rain fell that evening and night.

MAY 2   We followed up the railroad and went through the small burg, Cozad. Our travel was over muddy roads all day. A single-tree to the hack in which mother and we children were riding, was broken while crossing an irrigation ditch. At night we camped near Gothenberg.

MAY 3   Our journey from Kearney had been on the north side of the Platte River, on the Morman Trail. We then decided to again cross over the river to the Oregon Trail road. The wind blew a gale, making our crossing very disagreeable over the mile long bridge. At night we camped near a school house.

MAY 4   We found the roads heavy with sand. As a result, the decision was made to again cross the North Platte at North Platte town, to the Morman Trail road. The weather was cool and the wind blew.

MAY 5   This being Sunday, we rested. The weather was fine.

MAY 6-7   A man and his wife, Chris and Lena Bodewick (German Folk), who were enroute to Oregon, joined our crowd. They had a parrot that talked but was seemingly very timid. Later on they traded this bird for a horse as their team was growing weary and needed help to keep going. They also had three

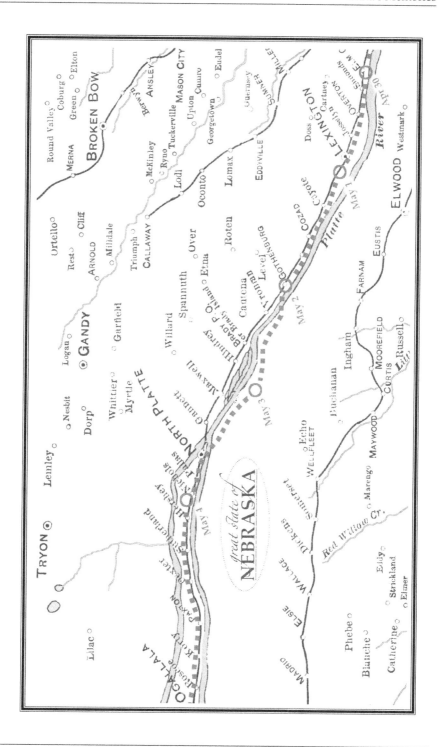

badgers that they captured along the way. We went through two small stations Sutherland and Hershey. We went through Paxton station and camped at Ogallala. The roads were heavy with sand. We children did not wish to walk as many sand toads were along the way.

MAY 8 We went through the town of Brule. We again crossed to the south side of the South Platte to avoid the sand. Our camp at night was on the Prairie. The weather was very warm with hot winds. A heavy gale and dust storm came our way.

MAY 9 We again crossed the South Platte to the north side at Big Springs. There we left the river, crossed over the hills and came to Lodge Pole Creek. We caught some fish there. We went through the town of Chappell and camped.

MAY 10 We went through Lodge Pole town and camped by the railroad near a section house. The weather was chilly. Ice was found in the water pail that night.

MAY 11 The weather was very cold. After going through the town of Sidney, we traveled twenty five miles west of there and camped.

MAY 12 We rested in camp till Monday morning. A number of tramps came begging for food. At night we camped by a mill. The menfolk caught some fish. We saw our first evergreen tree on the bluffs.

MAY 13 We went through three small towns, Potter, Dix, and Kimball. We traveled twenty-eight miles and camped.

MAY 14 We again drove a distance of twenty-eight miles and crossed the Nebraska line into Wyoming. We went through two small stations, Pine Bluffs and Egbert.

MAY 15 We went through Hillsdale station. We got our first

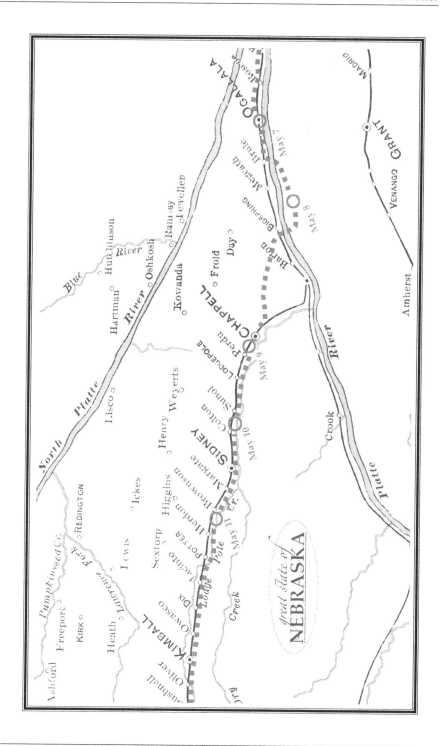

glimpse of the mountains in the afternoon. They resembled deep-blue clouds. This was a wonderful sight to us. The weather was so very cold that evening. We camped about eight miles east of Cheyenne.

MAY 16   Early morning found the ground white with snow. We went through Cheyenne and camped for dinner. The snow was falling and the wind was blowing a gale. We were so cold that we could scarcely eat our noonday meal around the campfire. We purchased a sheet-iron camp stove for our tent. (Austin had one). We had passed a number of graves by the roadside that day. Our camp that night was near the mountains.

MAY 17   We remained in camp and washed in the forenoon, then traveled to the mountains in the afternoon and camped at night by a high cliff of rocks. Some men on horseback came along driving a herd of horses down the mountain road. As some of our horses were not hobbled and had been turned loose that they might graze on the green grass, they too, ran with the herd and soon had disappeared. These men saw our camp and swiftly rode down the steep hillside, stopped our horses and brought them back to us.

There was real excitement in our camp. Chris took his two bird dogs and gun in search of game. He had gone a short distance back of the cliff when we heard the report of his gun. Soon Chris came carrying a large bobcat over his shoulder. He had found it feasting on a lamb. It had crouched ready for his dogs.

MAY 18   We traveled all day through the mountains and at night camped three miles east of Laramie on the Laramie Plain.

MAY 19   That Sunday was our rest day. The weather was cold and rainy.

MAY 20   We went through Laramie City. There we purchased a supply of provisions. The weather was cold and rain fell all day. Again we camped on the plains.

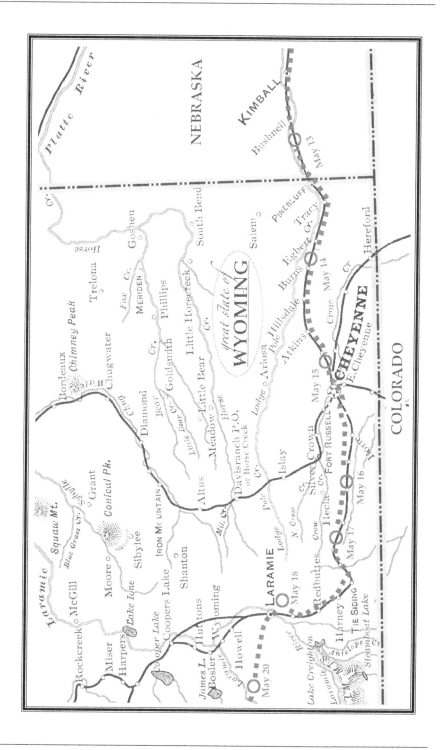

<u>MAY 21</u> We traveled until noon. We remained in camp until the next morning as the rain was falling.

<u>MAY 22</u> We traveled on for about three miles and crossed Rock Creek on a toll bridge, which cost us twenty-five cents per team. We stopped there until afternoon so that the roads might dry and be better for travel.

<u>MAY 23</u> We passed a trading point. That afternoon our way led up a canyon. We camped early that our horses might have a longer rest.

<u>MAY 24</u> We crossed the South Platte River and camped in the town of Saratoga at night.

<u>MAY 25</u> We crossed the river and started for Rawlins. We traveled until after dark in search of good water for ourselves and teams. Only alkali water could be found.

<u>MAY 26</u> Sunday was rest day. The wind blew all day.

<u>MAY 27</u> At Rawlins we purchased a supply of provisions. There we were misguided and took the wrong road to the north, causing us two extra days of travel. At night we camped on a creek with good grass for our teams.

<u>MAY 28</u> Our roads were heavy with sand all day. At night our camp was in a valley by a vacated stage station. There again the sand-toads caused despair to us children, as we were afraid of them. The northwest wind blew a gale and snow fell. That was a very cold night. Chris and Austin killed an antelope.

<u>MAY 29</u> We remained in camp as the snow fell most of the day.

<u>MAY 30</u> We traveled until noon and camped near Sand Creek.

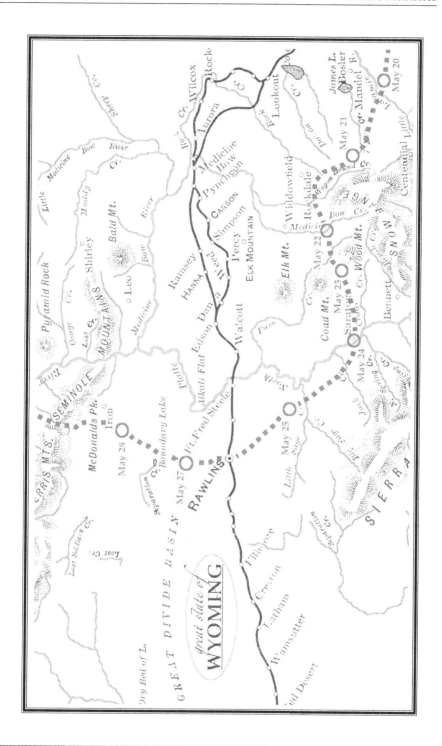

The rain fell in the afternoon, and the snow came down at night.Some of our group were not well, as they had eaten too much fresh antelope meat. Our beds were damp and we slept in wet garments. Our plight was despairing as we were many miles from a physician.

MAY 31 We did not travel in the forenoon as the roads were muddy. We went on in the afternoon and camped at night in the Sweetwater Valley. The weather was cold and the rain fell.

JUNE 1 We traveled on, and at noon camped near a ranch house. Austin killed an antelope. We camped near the Sweetwater that night.

JUNE 2 We remained in camp. The rain fell.

JUNE 3 We remained in camp. The rain continued to fall. At night we camped by the Sweetwater again.

JUNE 4 We traveled until ten o'clock and camped. As it was a warm sunny day, we washed and dried our clothes and bedding that had been wet for a weeks time. The rain had fallen and we had no opportunity to care for them. Chris killed another antelope, which again solved our meat problem.

JUNE 5 Another fine day. We traveled on and came to Rongis, a country trading post. Mother was ill all day.

JUNE 6 That was a windy day. We met a number of travelers leaving Oregon and Idaho going back east as they had become discouraged in the new country. At night we camped on the Sweetwater River again.

JUNE 7 That was another cloudy, snowy forenoon. We went through Lewiston, a mining town on the summit of the mountains. Another family joined our caravan, and traveled with us for some distance.

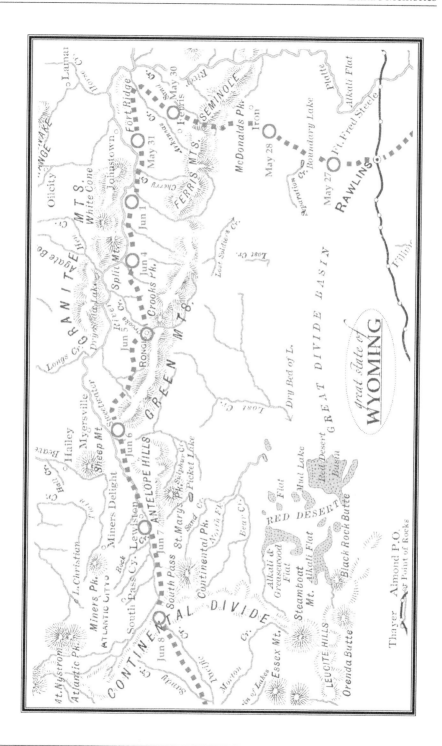

JUNE 8 That day was cold and chilly. We ate our noon lunch near the Sweetwater River. There we saw four soldiers' graves. At night our camp was by the small town of Pacific Springs. The water was not good. We paid two dollars for a sack of flour.

JUNE 9 The decision was made to travel that Sunday as we had remained in camp so much of the time on account of bad roads. We met a number of emigrants leaving the State of Washington enroute to Missouri. We crossed the Little Sandy River and camped.

JUNE 10 We crossed the Green River and traveled up the stream for about eight miles before camping. We were advised to lead our teams that they might drink from this stream, since a previous traveler had ridden his horse for water and had fallen into the river and drowned.

JUNE 11 We crossed the Green River on a ferry, which cost us $1.50 per team. That evening we camped on Slate Creek.

JUNE 12 That was a very warm day. The men folk went hunting as we had camped early. Our camp was in a small valley.

JUNE 13 That too, was a warm day. Our traveling was difficult as the roads were muddy and over a mountainous country. Our journey was up Hamsford Creek. After crossing that small stream, we camped.

JUNE 14 Again we crossed Hamsford Creek. The roads were rough. We met a traveler who had buried his brother in the mountains near the road we would travel. We crossed two mountain ranges. When descending the last one, into the valley below, we found the road so steep that it was necessary to fasten trees to the backs of our wagons to serve as brakes. We were frightened as we had never experienced anything like that before.

JUNE 15 We drove to Coksville and purchased a supply of

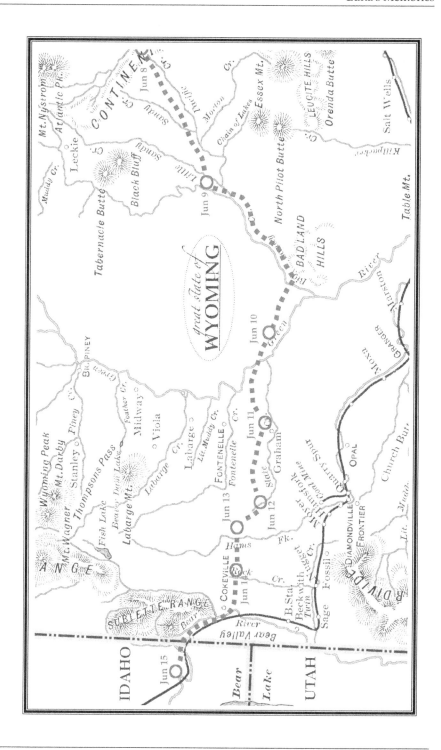

provisions as our food supply had run short. In the afternoon, we crossed from Wyoming into Idaho. After traveling up the railroad for some distance, we camped near Bear River.

JUNE 16   Early morning found the ground white with snow. The storm continued all day. The men folk caught a few fish.

JUNE 17   Our way was up a canyon that forenoon. In the afternoon we came to a beautiful valley. We passed through the town, Montpelier, and camped in a Morman settlement, which occupied most of the valley.

JUNE 18   We went through two Morman towns. Our journey was over rough roads all day. We had our teams shod at Soda Springs, where we camped.

JUNE 19   We went on in the afternoon. When evening came, we found that three of our horses were sick. They had drunk too much alkali water.

JUNE 20   We passed by a country store. At night our camp was on the Indian Reservation. There was good grazing for our teams.

JUNE 21   That was another very warm day. We camped early as we had found good grass and water. We saw Fort Hall which was erected in 1847. Indians were returning on horseback from a school picnic. Some were walking. We children had read stories of the Indians but had not seen them before. Our mother waited for us, as we were walking some distance behind and she thought that we would be frightened.

JUNE 22   We went through the town of Blackfoot. Chris Bodewick and wife, Lena, left us as they decided to go another way. We crossed the Snake River on a bridge. At night our camp was near an irrigation ditch.

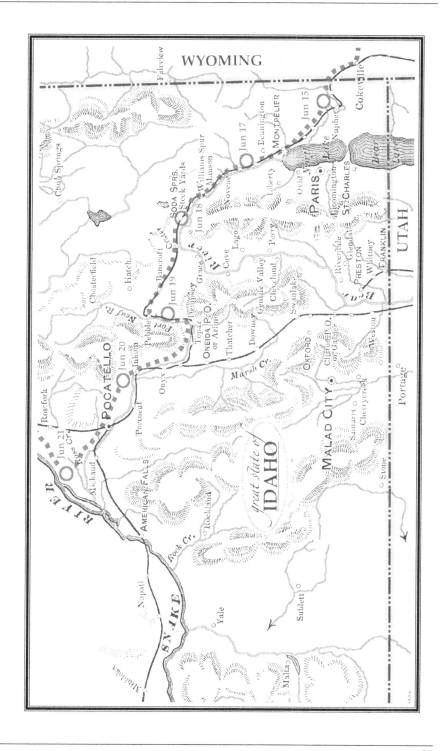

JUNE 23 Our journey was across a forty mile desert. We filled kegs and pails with water to drink.   After we had gone about twenty miles of distance, we purchased nine pailfuls of water for our teams. (We paid 25 cents per pailful.) A wagon laden with barrels of water was sent to meet travelers who were crossing this desert. The day was extremely warm and the roads were dusty. At night we came to the Big Lost River. Before reaching this river, our teams had sensed the water. That gave them courage to carry on. As they were warm and thirsty, we gave them but little water to drink at any one time. The extra family that had joined us, gave their horses all they wished to drink. This was a mistake as they became seriously ill and could not travel farther. We left them near a farm house.

JUNE 24   We drove about a mile to let our teams eat grass. After sixteen miles of travel during the afternoon, we camped near a trading center, where we got water for our horses.

JUNE 25   We found hot weather and a dust storm came at night. We camped in a valley filled with lava beds.

JUNE 26 Our way was in the valley with mountain peaks on one side of the road, and lava beds on the opposite side. The road wound its way around the foot of these mountains.   Snakes, ground-hogs, and owls inhabited these lava beds. The bones of animals could be seen in deep caves where they had fallen. Deep fissures in the lava could be seen.   We saw a large lake in the afternoon. Four emigrants' graves were near the road. Our camp at night was on Fish Creek.

JUNE 27 We went on and crossed the Little Wood River. Our way was through the mountains.   We did our washing that afternoon as the day was warm. The men folk caught some fish.

JUNE 28 We went through Belvue and crossed the Big Wood River. At night we camped in a valley. It was dry and dusty.

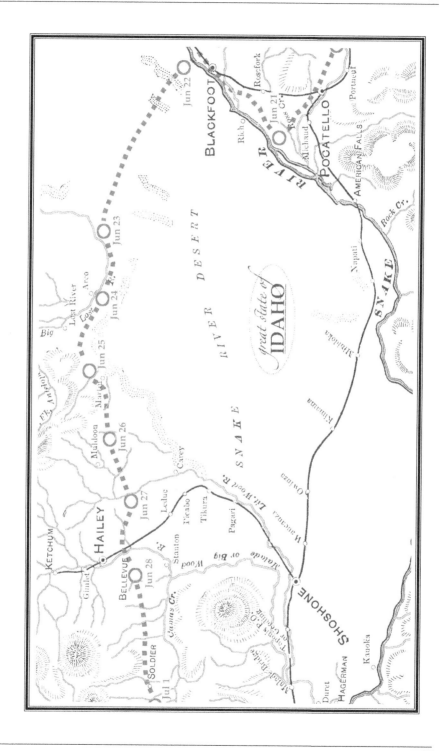

JUNE 29 Some clouds appeared and a bit of rain fell. We fished for three hours in vain.

JUNE 30 That day being Sunday, we did not travel. A few fish were caught.

JULY 1 We went through Soldier town, near Soldier Mountains and on across a creek of the same name. At night we camped by some soft mirt springs. Some of our horses had to be dug out of the mud when they were trying to get water to drink.

JULY 2 There were level roads during the forenoon, but in the afternoon, our way was among high mountains and rocks. We passed two country stores, Camas and Dixie.

JULY 3 That forenoon, our way was through the mountains. After noon we went down into the Snake River Valley. At night we camped near a ranch home where we found feed for our teams.

JULY 4 Some rain fell that day. Our mother had headache all day. We camped on a prairie. The large red crickets seemed to have taken possession of everything. The roads were covered with them. The weather was cool.

JULY 5 A heavy rain came just before we reached Boise. We bought a supply of provisions, after we had crossed the Boise River. Our camp at night was in a valley west of Boise. That was mother's 33rd birthday.

JULY 6 We traveled until noon. Then Austin and Henry decided to go and see Long Valley, *[McCall, Donnelly area]* sixty miles away on another route. We went on toward Palouse, Washington. We journeyed down to the Payette Valley and camped near Emmett, a small town.

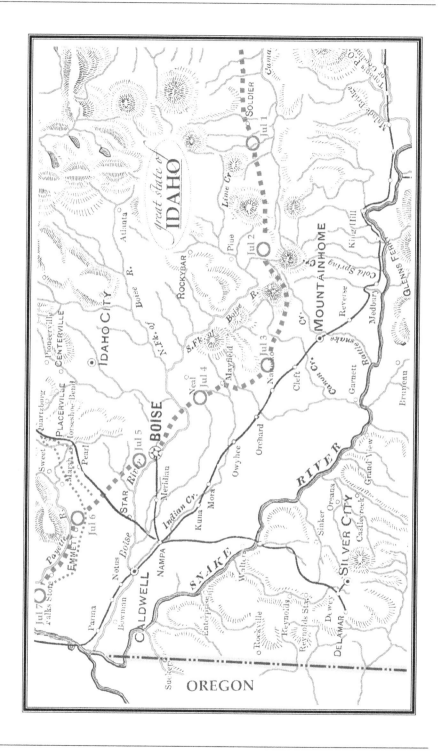

JULY 7   We passed through Emmett and went on down the Payette River all day.   When we camped at noon near a school house and saw young folk going to Sunday School, we wished we might go too.   There was some grass along the way for our teams. We traveled until night to find good feed for them.   We passed a country trading post.

JULY 8   We camped until noon as the horses needed rest. Father caught fourteen large fish.   To our surprise, we saw Austin and Henry coming in the distance.   They had changed their minds and decided to catch up with us.   There was a grand reunion, as we had been traveling alone since they left us.   We stayed in camp until the next day, as the men decided to catch more fish.   We got feed for our horses.

JULY 9   We went through two railroad stations, Payette and Weiser.   After crossing the Payette River, we saw some large Black and Cinnamon bears chained in a barn.   We were cautioned to not go near as they were wild.

JULY 10   We crossed the Snake River into Oregon on a ferry. It cost us twenty-five cents per team.   We then went over a new road that followed the bluffs of the river.   As there were so few places in this road that teams could pass, Nettie spent the forenoon walking ahead of our wagons to halt approaching teams.   We went through Huntington and camped.

JULY 11   We crossed the railroad sixteen times that day.   We passed a small station and crossed Burnt River.   There we caught more fish.   At night our camp was near a ranch where we got feed for our teams.

JULY 12   Our way was across the railroad seven times that day. We passed a small station.   The roads were very dusty.   We went through Baker City and camped.

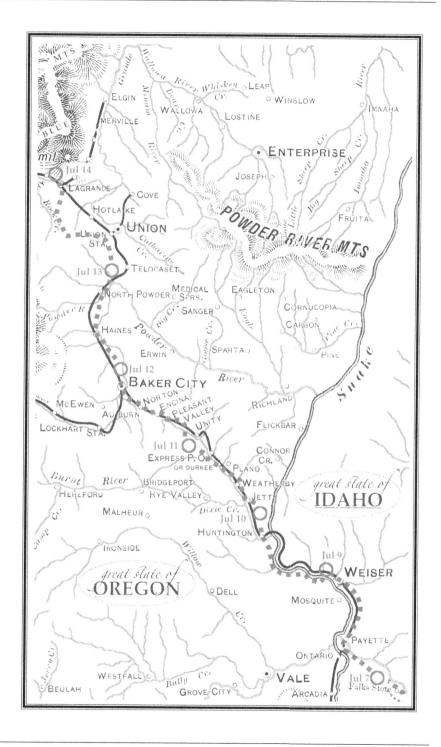

JULY 13 That was the second day in succession that we found dry and dusty roads. We went through Haines, a small village. We crossed the Powder River and camped in the Powder Valley.

JULY 14 La Grande, in the Grande Ronde Valley was the next town through which our road led us. The present road from Baker to La Grande had not been built at that time, as the swamps near La Grande made it necessary to ascend from the Powder Valley into the hills. There was no other way but to then cross the divide and into the Grande Ronde Valley. This descent is one to never be forgotten. The wheels were locked and the wagons slid over several hundred feet of crumbling rock to the valley below. We crossed the La Grande River and went through the town of the same name.

JULY 15 We went from the valley into the Blue Mountains and camped in a canyon to do our washing.

JULY 16 We traveled up these mountains all day. At evening we began a downward trend and camped near a toll-gate. We had gone fifty miles through heavy timber. We paid forty-five cents for pasture and toll.

JULY 17 In the forenoon, we went down the mountains and came into the Walla Walla Valley. After crossing the Walla Walla River, we crossed from Oregon into Washington State.

JULY 18 We went through Walla Walla and Dixie towns, and came to another small village and camped. Some rain fell that night.

JULY 19 Our road then was across the bluffs. They were dry and dusty most of the day. Father, Nettie, and Henry were sick that day. When we camped that night, we put our teams into a barn that had once been a stage station.

JULY 20 After we had gone twenty miles, we crossed the

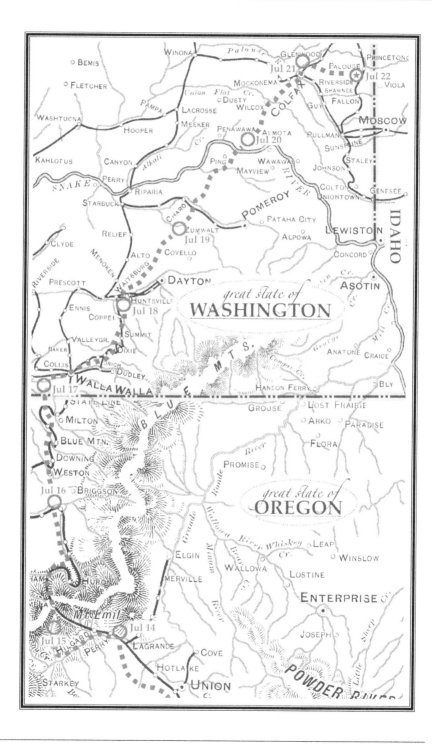

Snake River on a ferry which cost us fifty cents per team. At night we camped in a fruit orchard.

JULY 21 We went up a canyon road and came into the Palouse country. We went through the town of Colfax and then crossed the Palouse River.

JULY 22 We crossed the Palouse River again. As we were nearing our first destination, we stopped and prepared to go to the Columbus Ballard home for supper. We crossed the Palouse River again before reaching their home. We stretched our tents in their front yard and camped. We were happy that our first destination had been reached and that our long journey had come to an end. However, some of the children wished to travel on. (The Columbus Ballard family were friends who previously resided near Northbranch, Kansas.)

Epilogue

It had been eighty-nine days since we had left Northbranch, Kansas. We had traveled approximately 1600 miles. It had been a journey of hardship, but one to be remembered by all members of our party.

Austins and Henry remained at Ballard's for some time. After a few days, we went to Sprague, Washington, where Uncle Elias Ratcliff (father's brother) with his family resided. Later on we went to Davenport, Washington, where father's niece, Bessie Horwege and family lived, and still later to the home of his half-sister, Emily and her husband, Moultrie Davis and their family. They lived on a ranch near the Spokane River.

After a few days, we returned to the Columbus Ballard home and camped for about a week, before going to the home of the Jason Kellum family, who resided near Avon, Idaho. They, too, were friends from Northbranch, Kansas. Avon was located on Bear Creek which is twenty miles northeast of Moscow, Idaho. We pitched our tent for three weeks in Jason's yard. Father went away to harvest.

We soon moved into a house which was known as the "Greenwood Home", not far away. The next year, we moved into the Dave Parks house which was two miles south of Avon. There we children fished for trout in Bear Creek.

We were on this ranch for eighteen months before moving to the Lapwai Reservation in 1897.

We reached Woodland, Idaho in early spring and made camp on the Enoch Kenworthy homestead which was one fourth mile from the Austin S. George home. (Enoch too, was a Northbranch farmer.). *[Enoch Kenworthy's homestead was directly across the road (to the north) from where the church parsonage is now.]*

Austin had filed on an homestead in March 1896, and had moved there in June of the same year. Henry was with them.

Our destination had then been reached. We had traveled approximately 2000 miles. John F. and Mary Ellen Hodson (our grandparents) and family had traveled from Northbranch, by team to our home at Avon, Idaho in 1896. They had moved to Big Bear Ridge, twelve miles south of there and then to Woodland with us in 1897. Irma and Earl Mills (their grandchildren) had come from Kansas to their home before moving to Woodland.

Enos Adamson and sons, Clarence and Elmer, also traveled from Kendrick, Idaho to Woodland with us. They had previously come West from Iowa. They had purchased cows, and they and Enoch and Rachel Kenworthy were the early cheesemakers in the Woodland community.

As had been planned, a new community was being formed on the Lapwai Reservation. Woodland was named by Austin.

The Sunday School, as well as spelling school was being held in their home. He (Austin) gave an acre of land on which a log school house was to be built.

The Woodland postoffice was soon located in the Isaac C. George home.

The Columbus (Dump) Ballard family, the Jason Kellum family, the Isaac George family, May Haskins, Oscar and his wife Lizzie (Ballard) Dillon, (Lizzie had taught a subscription school), Allen Knight, John Haskins, the Frank Davis family, Fred Limbacker, Harley, O.C. and D.V. Lansing, Zenas Carey George family, Hal Emery, (all from Kansas) had settled there. Other Kansas farmers who came later on were, the Nathan Hollingsworth family, the Dave Haskins family, the William Carson family, Levi Craven, the John George family, the Oscar Lansing family, the George Sanders family, the Benjamin White family, Miles Moon, the Daniel Moon family, the Q.V. Moon family, the Daniel Bundy family, the Fred Jay family, Peninah Jay and Arthur Sanders family.

Other settlers came and all worked together to make a prosperous community. Most of the early settlers there from Kansas were a modest, peaceful folk, known as Friends (Quakers).

Some are at rest in the Woodland neighborhood cemetery. Many of their children live and have proven that their parents' efforts were not in vain. *[This sentence resonates deep within me, as I am one who has benefited from the hard work and sacrifice of these settlers...my ancestors. Not in vain, nor taken for granted.]*

Those of our party, now deceased and buried in the Woodland cemetery are;

Thomas Elwood Ratcliff, born April 14, 1851, died April 27, 1922.
Martha Adella Ratcliff, born July 5, 1862, died March 19, 1900.
[Notice that Edna's mother died three years after arriving in Woodland at the young age of 37.]
Austin S. George, born December 12, 1863, died April 29, 1908.
Mabel (George) Finney, born November 13, 1884, died September 28, 1935.
Lydia George, born 1894, died Oct. 15, 1901.
Henry Haskins, buried elsewhere.

CHAPTER FOUR
June Hodson (1921-2004)

June Phyllis Hodson, 1939

[This account, by one of my cousins, is an excellent summation of the move to Idaho and surrounding circumstances. June was the daughter of Estella, Ora's sister. June lived a hop, skip and a jump down the road from her grandmother Sarah in a house later owned by Glen and Verla Simler.

June attended the Woodland School for Grades 1-10. During this time, children at the school completed two high school grades in Woodland before they went on to Kamiah or Kooskia for the last two years and graduation. June graduated from Kamiah High School in 1939 as the Valedictorian.

June passed away on June 1, 2004, in Orofino.

This article was originally printed in the June 1986 edition of <u>Good Old Days</u> magazine. It is being reprinted here with the permission of <u>Good Old Days</u> magazine. I have corrected a few typos. It was written by Arlene Baker as told by June Hodson Schoeffler.]

Down An Awful Steep Hill

An 1895 Journey to Idaho

Part I

The steep hills of that little girl's diary have long been tamed, and a summer trip from Kansas to the Northwest today is hardly more than an outing, as my neighbor would say. I doubt if either of us would choose a covered wagon for that "outing," load it with all our possessions, including a flock of kids, and spend eighty-nine days in total discomfort following a dirt trail across five states!

That's exactly what my grandparents did in 1895, and this is the story of that journey.

Fortunately, two diaries, several letters and many mementoes survive, because Grandma George, as we called her in later years, seldom mentioned that covered wagon journey. There was a natural reticence on her part, but I also suspect we did not ask the right questions. The "roots awareness" of today was still far in the future. To her, I'm sure it counted as just another link in a long chain of events, for her 94 years took her from the time of the Civil War and sod-shanty homesteads to the age of earth-circling satellites.

Born in Iowa in 1864, by 1871 she was pioneering with her preacher-parents in a sod house on the Kansas-Nebraska border. In 1882, she became the wife of a young Quaker farmer, and by 1895 she was the mother of four little girls and about to "pioneer" again. That year the young couple sold their holdings in

Northbranch, Kansas, loaded the wagons, and on a bright April afternoon, set out for the homestead lands of Northern Idaho. She was thirty-one years old.

"Grandma George" was Sarah Jeanette (Nettie) Haskins, the daughter of John J. and Nancy (Edgerton) Haskins, both of whom were ministers of the United Brethren Church. The neighbors said of Great-Grandfather Haskins, "He was verbose and vociferous when he got warmed up, and everybody within a half-mile could hear his preachin." (Born in 1838, he was still going strong in 1918, when he was gored by a bull and died a few days later.) The family homesteaded on Star Creek, near Guide Rock, Nebraska in 1871. Nettie grew up there and married Austin Sherman George, whose parents, Isaac and Hannah, were farming in nearby Northbranch, a small Kansas community with strong Quaker roots.

By 1895, the years of drought, grasshoppers and dust storms had already sent many Kansas farmers to the Northwest in search of new farm land and a more kindly climate. Nettie and Austin George decided it was time to make the same move.

They would make the trip with their friends, Thomas Elwood and Martha (Hodson) Ratcliff and their five girls. Nettie's Uncle Henry Haskins decided to go with them and readied his wagon and his two grays, Lorne and Fannie. (Martha had a nine-year old brother, Harley Hodson, who made the trip in 1897. Harley and five-year-old Estella of this story eventually became my parents.)

Grandma George's "shopping list" for that wagon trip was a four-page order to Montgomery Ward, dated March 8, 1895-- twelve yards of dark moleskin shirting ($1.50), two pairs of brown overalls ($1.00), one 7 x 9 tent ($5.85), another, 9 x 12 ($8.00), twelve yards of indigo print, feather ticking, shotgun shells, powder and much more. The total bill was $29.64.

Tucked into Grandma's trunk was a much-cherished gift from her Northbranch neighbors, a blue and white quilt top with their names written on tiny slips of paper and pinned to the quilt. I have it today, just as she received it at her "going away" party on April 19, 1895, pieced and signed by Elizabeth Kivett, Sarah and Silvia Hadley, Ruth and Mahlon Lamb, D.W. and M. E. Pearson and so many, many others.

Five days after the party, the wagons gathered. Farms had been sold, goods auctioned, their "goodbyes" said - the Ratcliff girls, Edna, age 12, Dosha 10, Alma 8, Orpha 5, and Olive 2, were dressed and waiting. Grandma George had her girls in new dark moleskin dresses. Mabel, age 11, Ora 9, Estella 5 (my mother), and the baby Lydia, 18 months, also had new blue "hankies" as Ora called them, tied around their heads. With so many girls, Grandma wanted to keep track of her own. Edna Ratcliff and Ora George were to be the journey's diarists and one of Ora's first entries was, "Nine girls. Not one boy!"

Grandpa's two mules, Dick and Daisey, were hitched to the George wagon. "Old Seal" was to be the riding horse, and Grandpa took his yellow dog, "Curly." The Ratcliffs had two wagons and their shepherd dog, "Spud."

On April 24, 1895, the wagons pulled out of the yard - three men, two women and nine little girls, headed for the old Oregon Trail and Idaho.

Their destination "out west" was to be the home of ex-Northbranch neighbors, the Columbus Ballard family, then living on the Idaho border in Palouse, Washington. That first afternoon might have been a "trial run" with the wagons; Grandma and Grandpa George drove to the elder George's farm, while the Ratcliffs stayed with a cousin nearby. Both men lightened their wagons considerably and left much to be shipped to Idaho later. (I don't know what agreement was made on what would be left behind, but it wasn't Grandma's Kansas rosebush. She planted it in the yard of her new home in 1896, and when we built our home in 1949, she gave us a "start." The old Kansas rose still blooms profusely every spring along our side fence.)

The two families met the next day and camped the first night at Red Cloud, Nebraska, a few miles from Grandma's childhood home. The second campsite was near Bladen, where Edna noted a family named Sweltzer came to visit, "and their little daughter, Minnie, entertained us by singing a song."

On April 29, the diaries record the wagons crossing the Platte near Kearney, Nebraska, in search of better roads. It was here that

Spud caused much consternation and crying among the little girls. The wagons rumbled across the narrow bridge while Spud went down for a drink. Seeing the wagons on the other side, he panicked and struggled to swim across the wide river. Spud finally made it, but not before he scared the girls half to death.

The two girls recorded every town the wagons passed through, as well as every campsite. Ora kept a meticulous account of the price of supplies along the trail. (Arithmetic lessons?) They noted rivers, toll bridges, the weather, dismal, with much rain, snow and unexpected cold, and the long sandy stretches inhabited by "sand toads," which the girls hated. (They were afraid of them, and were allowed to ride the wagons through the "bad" sections.) To be continued.

Part II

We know from Ora's diary that butter ranged from 10-25 cents a pound on the trip, baled hay 40-45 cents and a sack of flour in Big Springs, Nebraska was 90 cents. Down the road in Lodgepole they bought a wooden butter bucket for 15 cents. Ora's granddaughter, Lorene Johnson, is still using the same bucket today.

On May 6, not far from Cozad, Nebraska, Chris and Lena Bodewick, headed for Oregon, joined the wagons. When the travelers left the old Oregon Trail and took the shorter route across southern Wyoming, it was Grandpa and Chris who provided fresh meat, usually antelope, for the cooking pots.

They camped near Lodgepole on May 10th, and Edna recorded, "chilly weather and ice on the water pail," and a few days later, near Cheyenne, the first snow. On May 15th, the diaries mention the first glimpse of mountains: "they resemble deep blue clouds, a wonderful sight to us." They also meant rain, snow and mud, as both girls would later record.

West of Cheyenne, the girls note the first of many emigrant graves, and the next day one diary tells of the great excitement in camp: "Chris had taken his two bird dogs in search of game, and instead had come back with a 'large bobcat' over his shoulder."

Through late May and early June, they fought the rain, mud

and cold, until finally forced to call a halt north of Rawlins, Wyoming, and wait for a warm day to dry out the bedding, their clothing and themselves. The diaries mention passing illnesses in the families, but not until May 30th, after several days of terrible cold, does a note of fear creep into the accounts. Many in the party "were not well, our plight was despairing as we were many miles from a physician." What ever caused the sickness eventually subsided and the wagons were able to continue on to the Sweetwater River.

Wagon travel in the 1890's was not easy, especially with nine little girls and the ever-present threat of illness. By the mid-90's, however, the old Oregon Trail across Nebraska was peppered with small towns and farming communities from which to buy food and supplies. But through Wyoming and Idaho, finding water for the stock presented a very real problem: the girls wrote that the horses were often sick from alkali water and on a forty-mile stretch of desert in Idaho, the men pay $2.25 for nine buckets of fresh water for the animals, and were "lucky to get that." (The diaries also noted the generosity of many farmers who not only provided water, but let them camp in their meadows to allow the stock to graze.)

Ora writes of an event that frightened them all on June 15th. Just before entering Cokeville, on the Wyoming-Idaho border, they "came down an awful steep hill and had to tie trees to the back of the wagons - Mama (Grandma George) and all nine of us girls walked down ahead of the teams." When they finally pulled into Cokeville after that harrowing experience, Ora remembered to record that they bought "a quarter's worth of apples." This was the first steep hill, but not the last. Grandpa George evidently became an expert on using trees as brakes on the wagons, for in his letters to his parents, he included drawings and specifications for the blacksmith in Northbranch to use in forging certain pieces of ironwork "that will make the job easier for you when you come out next year."

Several days after "the awful steep hill" at Cokeville, Ora writes they stopped in Soda Springs, Idaho to get the mules shod ($2.75) and "Mama sat in the wagon and pieced quilt blocks."

The Bodewicks left the group three days later in Blackfoot. The two families and Uncle Henry continued to Arco, across to Boise, up to Payette and Weiser, and on July 10th, they crossed the Snake River on the Ferry (25 cents per team), and were in Oregon. They followed a new road along the bluffs which was so narrow, Nettie had to spend the whole morning walking far ahead to warn oncoming teams. The girls spent a great deal of time on the trip walking behind the wagons (except through the "sand toad" stretches!) and undoubtedly some of them walked with her along this new trail.

[Sand Toads, also known as Woodhouse Toads, are fairly large toads approaching six inches in length. Maybe the size scared the girls or the stories of handling toads and getting warts. None of which would scare our intrepid granddaughter Tenley, our budding biologist. She will grab or hold nearly anything; much to her mother's chagrin.]

By now, they had been seventy-seven long days and nights on the trail, and were just twelve days from "home". They passed through Baker (Oregon) and on July 12th, "along terribly dry and dusty roads," then on through Haines, the Powder Valley, LaGrande, and finally six days out of Baker, they were in Walla Walla, Washington.

A few more dusty and dry days, according to the girls, and at long last, eighty-nine days out of Northbranch, they pulled into the Ballard yard in Palouse on July 22, 1895. They were home, almost.

Grandma and the girls stayed in Palouse (the girls went to school) until June of 1896, when Grandpa returned after filing on homestead land ten miles out of Kamiah, Idaho. He had spent the winter and spring clearing eleven acres, planting three vegetable crops, building a two story log cabin and writing to his parents and brothers urging them to come to this new land. *[Picture on following page: View of the Clearwater River valley seen from halfway up the Woodland grade and looking back towards the present town of Kamiah. This was the view, 1889-1892, and would have been very similar to what the Georges saw in 1896 when they moved to Woodland. Photographer E. Jane Gay, courtesy Idaho State Historical Society, 63-221-047.]*

Then he brought Grandma and his girls to the new settlement he had named "Woodland".

Grandma George was to spend the rest of her long life in Woodland. Lydia died of scarlet fever in 1901 and Grandpa in 1908, when smallpox swept the settlement. In 1910, she built a lovely two-story frame house from the plans she and Grandpa George hand made, and in the years following, she raised the three girls, managed her prosperous farm and served the community as mid-wife, working along with her mother-in-law Hanna George.

When she died in 1959, just short of her 95th birthday, she was surrounded by eighty-four grandchildren, great-grandchildren and great-great-grandchildren. Ora's grandson, Leonard Bacon lives with his family in Grandma George's lovely old Woodland home today.

Woodland's First Store

John Haskins log cabin was one of Woodland's few historical places. It was built in Grandma Nettie Georges back yard, just beside the road which leads from grandma's house to ours. He had put an addition on the cabin and made it into a store for the pioneers.

After Great Grandpa Haskins returned to Guide Rock, Nebraska to live, the sides of his house was torn off and used for other sheds or for repairs on chicken houses or barn and etc. Some of the logs were used for other things on the farm. There was only this small log room left which Grandma Nettie used for a hog shed in the days of my youth. Grandpa Haskins had originally built it for his wood shed.

I can recall how Keith and I liked to climb on the roof and play until Grandma would make us get down. She was afraid we would fall and get hurt so we waited until she was milking or some place where she couldn't see us and then we would sneak up on the roof and enjoy looking down on our small world.

The little piglets below us were our enemies and we had imaginary battles and killed most of them before Grandma would spy us. Woe be unto us if we had really hurt any of her pigs!!

It seems we weren't the only ones who thought the small cabin would make an ideal place to play; however this was in later years after Grandma had taken all her pigs to market. Faye and Nettie Mae Anderson decided it would make a wonderful play house, but they changed their minds when Grandma scolded them for climbing over her fence.

It appears that sometimes grandchildren can be a trial for Grandmothers.

June Hodson Schoeffler

Grandma Bacon's Baptism

Mrs. Anna Bacon was Harold Bacon's grandmother. He was the only child of Ora and Fred Bacon. They lived a short distance from us so Harold, Ray and Pearl were always together. Therefore; we also called her "Grandma Bacon", although she was not our relative.

Her son, Fred Bacon married Ora George who was my mother's sister. Anna Bacon's daughter, Winifred married my Dad's brother, Lauren Hodson.

One time while I was visiting Kathryn Schlader she told me about Grandma Bacon's baptism at Pardee, Idaho. When the date was set for the community baptism, Grandma Bacon discovered her apparel would not be appropriate for baptizing. She was a sweet lady but quite large and very modest. She knew that after submersion her dresses would cling to her body and reveal her curves and bulges which she wished to conceal from the audience on the river bank.

She didn't waste any time sending for ten yards of unbleached muslin and when the order arrived she made herself an ankle length gown and gathered it at the neck. Kathryn said when Grandma Bacon stood up she looked like a walking tent.

They entered the river, which was high and swift and of course the current caught Grandma's dress and lifted it up like a balloon. She became panic-stricken and lost her balance and grabbed for the minister. While the two supporters were trying to calm her, the minister had his arms around her trying to hold her dress down and she was pushing him away with one hand and attempting to hold her gown down with the other.

The two men lost their footing and all were splashing around in the cold water, trying to get Grandma to shore. Everyone spent several anxious moments while the other men rushed down the bank to help Grandma back on dry land. I have often wondered if they ever got her baptized!

Written as told to me by Kathryn Schlader - JHS -

Anna Elisabeth Doane, "Grandma Bacon"

[Grandma Bacon's sturdy old rocking chair sits in my living room. If you ever come for a visit and find me sitting in Grandma's rocking chair giggling; I may not be ready for the old folks home, I could be remembering this story!]

❖

CHAPTER FIVE
Austin & Sarah George (1862-1908) & (1864-1959)

Austin, Sarah and girls in Kansas, shortly before the trip to Idaho.

[Austin and Sarah married on December 13, 1882, and promptly began the business of making girls. Mabel arrived in 1883, Ora in 1886, Estella

in 1889 and finally Lydia in 1893. As you will notice in the letters that follow, Lydia seemed to be a sickly child. She eventually died in Woodland in 1902 at the age of eight.

Mabel married Frank Finney in 1902, Ora married Fred Bacon, and Estella married Harley Hodson. The Ora-Fred and Estella-Harley union was a double ceremony in Lewiston on December 21 of 1911.

At her birth, Sarah was named Sarah Jeanett Haskins. As families are want to do, short nicknames develop. Sarah was known by her family as "Nettie", based most likely on a derivative of Jeanett. Since she is referred to as such by family, community and friends, she will primarily be known as "Nettie" moving forward in this manuscript.

As you have read, Austin and Nettie arrived in Palouse, Washington in July 1895. Austin promptly found work in nearby Pullman during the harvest. The three letters that follow are letters between Austin and Nettie as Austin worked during the grain harvest in nearby Pullman, preparing for that eventual trip to homestead in Idaho.]

From Nettie to Austin, August 14, 1895

Palouse
Aug 14, 1895

Dear Austin

We are all well, hope you are the same. Well we are getting alonge all right. We havent had time to get lonesome, for the fruit. We have picked 152 boxes of rasberries since you left and carried our share home on the horses. Willcox quit taking their milk to town. We have washed today and made catchup and done lots of other work.

Belle is writing to Lizzie.

There was a team coming down the road today. I heard Stella say to the girls, I wish that was Papa dont you? Baby says Papa is away.

We got the letter from your father. I gave it to Uncle *[Henry]*, I guess he has it with him. I will tell you what he said. The goods weighed 554 just as we left them and it would cost $2.40 a hundred if we took the risk of shiping ourselves, and if we put it in there care it would be 1/2 more. So Add *[Kellum]* said whenever the goods was receipted that was all right, they would haft to see to them so we took the risk. He said they would haft to box the trunk. Uncle sent for them Saturday.

Well, we have big times, dog fites and such-like. Will close for this time, after 6 o'clock and supper to get. I havent built a fire in the tent since you left. Write soon.

From Nettie to Austin

The 15th

Add was down last night. He wrote for the things for the gun. It will cost 60 cts with out postage. Mabel will take the letters to the Office. We thought we had better send 10 cts for postage. Belle got a letter from Lizzie. Will send it down there. She said things was getting dry there. Will close.

From Nettie to A.S.G.

From Nettie to Austin, August 28, 1895

Palouse, Wash
Aug 28, 1895

Dear Austin

I reced your letter last eavening. Was glad to hear from you once more, the time seamed long till we heard from you. Lyda was real sick yesterday and last night, is better now, she had diarrhea and high feaver. The rest is well as common.

We got a letter from your father, one from Dave *[Haskins, Nettie's brother]* and Uncle one from Laura *[Nettie's sister]*. She said some fields was as dry as this time last year, garden stuff all dried up.

Your father rote, Uncle dident send money enuff so I got on Seal, went to town, saw the agent and Mr. Boon. They said it would be all right shiped in owners risk so I sent $12.00 more. He said have them sent to Garfield so they wouldent have to be transfured, so I did. I didnt know what to do.

What are we going to do about the fruit? Can get peaches 35 cts a box. Write and let me know, fruit is going like hot cakes. I have some of Uncle's money, dont like to use it but have used some. Got Lyda shoes.

Seal is doing well, had chance to hire him out for 50 cts a day but thought best not to.

Yes I rote to Laura on Sunday after you left. I will send Dave letter. I want you to answer it rite away.

Well we are getting along well, no more dog fites. We would

like to see you real well but if you keep well and can stand the work stay, Cranks or no Cranks. Now I want you to wright rite away and let me know about the fruit. Will close for now.

From Nettie to Austin G.

Baby took a big Cry for Milk to day

Austin and Sarah, circa 1882

From Austin to Nettie, September 24, 1895

Pullman
Sept 24, 1895

We are done threashing and are halling wheat to get our pay.
Wont be home for 5 or 7 days I dont expect. We are going to stay
til we get our money or bust. Will send you a postal order for
$5.00 so you can get what you need. We are well and hope you
are the same. Yours,

Austin S. George

Editor's Notes

[Sometime in March of 1896, Austin came to the Kamiah area to find his special place in this world. He undoubtedly spent considerable time and travel trying to find the best piece of land...that one exceptional place.

After the land was selected, he had the mammoth job of building a cabin, clearing land, planting crops, etc. before he could bring Nettie and the girls to their new home. As a home builder and worker bee, I marvel at how much he was able to accomplish in such a short time.

The following are letters between Austin and Nettie during this time. In the first letter to Nettie, he describes the land he ultimately chooses to settle on in Woodland. I particularly appreciate his description of the "bluff".

The letters contain several facts of interest to me.   First, Austin believed Woodland was off the Nez Perce Indian reservation, which is an error.   Much of Woodland, including his homestead, lies just inside the boundaries of the reservation.   Secondly notice the spelling of Kamiah without the final "h".   Early maps of the period often show the spelling as "Kamia", consistent with Austin's spelling.

All other consideration aside, this was an uncommonly difficult period. Both struggling to keep food on the table, working from daylight to dark and missing each other.]

From Austin to Nettie, March 20, 1896

Kamia, March 20 1896

(to Nettie)

We are all well and able to eat. We got here last Tuesday noon. We went across the river to look at that land that Robberts told Uncle about and we found it as good as he represented it. We will start over this morning with the wagon.

It is about 12 miles from Kamia. Good roads after we get up the bluff but that is a terror. We had an awful time getting here the roads were so bad. Jason stalled on level ground and it took 8 horses to pull him out.

We can all get good land out side the Reservation. Plenty of fine timber and watter. I will get som cabbage and tomato seeds and sow before I leave. We think we can start home the fore part of next week.

There is lots of grouse and pheasants over there. We have had good weather most of the time. Sprinkled some night before last and some last night and is cloudy this morning. Wel this is all this time. I dont know whether I wil write any more or not as I wont have any chance to get it to the Office till we start home. Yours, A.S. George

From Nettie to Austin, April 21, 1896

Palouse, Apr 21 1896

Dear Austin

I will write a little. We are all well except Baby. Mabel sprained her left arm at the elbo. She is better now. She (Lyda) said tell Papa Mabel broke her arm. She said tell Pappa Diddy fell down. *[Lydia, as a toddler, was apparently pronouncing her name as "Diddy".]*

Well I got 4 letters Saturday eavening. I will send the mens letters and your Mothers. I cant send all this time.

Well I have saw Dumps *[Ballard]* folks ever day since you left. Belle *[Ballard]* and Lizzie *[Dillon]* was here and stayed all day Sat. The children and I went over there Sun. And Belle and Lizzie and I went to preachen at 3 o'clock, then Add, Belle and Lizzie went to Hamiltons yesterday, then Add and them was here for supper tonight.

Add said tell you he heard an old bob white this morning and if you wanted to hear it you would haft to come over. They want us to come over there to morrow. I don't know whether we will go or not. Add is going to the Office to morrow. He hasent heard from the boys yet.

Our hens is drying up. We got 2 eggs today. Add and Mabel went hunting, got phesent and grouse. We had them for supper.

Well the boys *[Austin's brothers]* write like they were coming. Don't write encouragingly or we will have more than we can handle, for if they wait till after corn is layed by to come with team there will be no harvest or nothing for them to do. I think some of the boys had ought to stay with Father. He is apt to get sick any time.

I will close for this time. Write and tell us all about your trip and how the roads are and how you are geting alonge. Baby fusses for you to come home when we don't say anything to her.

From N.G. To A. George

Austin, circa 1880

Postcard from Austin, April 23, 1896

Apr 23 -96
Kamia, Idaho

We got here at 1 o'clock today. Got along as wel as we expected. The roads across the mountain was bad. It rained quite a shower last evening. Tell Add that Hillsides is all right. Write as soon as you get this and let me know how you are getting along. I wil write a letter as soon as we get straitened around. Write soon.

Austin

From Nettie to Austin, April 28, 1896

Palouse, Wash.
Apr 28 - 96

Dear Austin

I will write you a few lines. For goodness sake what is the mater, we havent heard from you since you left. This is my last till I hear from you.

It is raining now. Belle and Lizzie went to town Friday. They walked down to Mr. Hues in the morning, stayed till after dinner, then went to Mr. Andersons and stayed there till Sat eavening and came out home with Evert. I started to town Sat. Got to Hues, it go to raining so I stayed there till the shower was over, then I came back home. So I went yesterday afternoon, thought I would here from you shure. I got to Mr. Hues, stoped to rest so Mrs. Hues hitched up and took me.

I got a letter from your folks. I will send it to you. I got a letter from W. C. George. I will send it but I wrote and told him when you started and when you thought you would be back. I thought it would be so long before he could get a letter from you.

What do you think about the boys starting so late? Dont you think they will have trouble to get watter some places and do you think they could get work that late, that is to amount to anything. They say Ben Wall is coming to. If they come they want our tent and our wagon cover. I dont think we can spare them, do you? If they come they will count on making their home with us I expect. Mother wants you to write and let them know what you think about starting so late. I dont think it best, do you?

Mabel is over to Belles helping make soap. Lizzie is haveing a time with her head. The rest of us is well as common but Oh so lonesome. It has quit raining. If it dont rain any more the girls is going to get Mr. Howells pony and take this to the Office this after noon and see if we can here from you. Belle and Lizzie was here and stayed all night Sunday night. I haven't bin there since last Wednesday. I have bin there twice since you left. Belle wants me to come over this after noon.

Ora went to catch the poney but they couldent catch it so they are going a foot.

Write and tell us when the mail leaves there. You told me but I have forgot. Lyda says Papa is far, far away. Well I will close for this time.

Mabel has just come from Belles. She said Lizzie was quite sick. They are going to send for some medasine. It is just her head is all I guess that ailes her.

Now I want you to write every time the mail leaves there. Let us know how you are getting along. The girls will write next time. We are getting along all right with the chores.

From Nettie George to Austin

From Austin to Nettie, May 14, 1896

Kamiah
May 14, 1896

Dear Nettie and Children

I will try and ans your letter dated Apr 28, which I received last Monday, the 11th, which is all the letters I have got from you except the one Add brought, and this makes four times I have written to you. What is the rip you dont write oftener.

Wel I have been plowing the garden and planting potatoes to day. It has quit raining quite so much but is still quite cool. Don't know when we wil have summer. It rains a little, then snows a little and then quits a little. It has been so wet we couldn't make any headway with our work. I have got my ground plowed for wheat. Wil take three or four days to finish Dumps.

I dont know when we will get started home but I expect it wil be a couple of weeks yet, and we couldent get back if we were there as the roads are so bad.

We are all wel and hope you the same. Add is going to the office tomorrow. The mail gets here on Mon & Fri and goes out on Tues & Sat. Wel I haven't any news to write so Good-Bye. Write two or three times a week and I wil write as often as I can get it to the Office.

Austin

May 15

Wel it rained and snowed last night and is stil cloudy this morning so I wil write some more. It seems like a long, long time since I saw you.

I was over to Jasons *[Kellum]* last night and I wanted Willy to come home with me. He said if Lyda was here he would go shure.

I answered Fathers letter you sent me by Add but aint answered the boys yet. I dident think it would be right for both of them to come and leave Father and Mother alone as they are liable to get sick and would be helpless if both got down at once.

We wil have to use our tent and cover till we get a house, and I wil have to take the cover when I go harvesting and I dont think we can spare them.

Did the catalog Eddie and I sent for come there. The small one came all right but the big one aint come yet. The papers are coming all right.

Our tomato plants aint doing any good, it has been so cool. It looks some like clearing up and Add thinks he wil go the Office so I wil close for this time. You said that your letter was the last till you heard from me. I think it was about your <u>first</u>. Write soon and often. As ever,

Austin to Nettie & the Children

From Nettie to Austin, May 15, 1896

Palouse, Wash
May 15, 1896

Dear Austin

I will try to write some more to you. We are all well. Hope you are the same. I got your card today. This is the third time I have wrote to you. I suppose you have got my seckond letter before this so that will avoid a <u>racket</u>. I got your letter one week ago yesterday. Lizzie and I walked down to town that day and back again (yes and down to the depot too). She thought maby their box of goods was there. They wasent. We got home a little after noon. We waited for the morning mail. We are practicing walking. We dident know but what we would haft to walk to our new homes. You don't know how we keep watch of the Office to here from you. It seamed like a longe time till we heard from you. It seames long from one letter to the next. Belle and Lizzie has bin here and stayed 6 nights with us.   They were here last night. Lizzie and Ora went to town today with Reggie.

Well we were slap dab out of flour. I sent by Mr. Hamilton and got 50 lbs. I tell you I would like to see you coming. We are out of meat, money and nearly everything else except milk and butter. The cow is doing better than she did when you left. She gives a 2 gal jar full of a night. I wish you had the milk that I haft to throw out. I feal like you dont have much to eat for you havent got milk and butter. I have bin letting Belle have milk and butter. They are just out of flour and their men never left them any money. I told them I woud devide with them. Our hens havent laid hardley any since you left. I have had 7 hens wanted to set.

I took 50 cts and got the girls (4) one pair of stockings apiece. Then I bought 10 cts worth of envelopes. I got a dishpan for 15 cts and I have got a quarter yet. We can get along all rite if we have flour (when we are alone).

Rain, I should say it has rained nearley every day since Add left till this week. Since the moon changed it has bin better. It hails or snowes a little ever day, the wind has bin blowing some. The roads is better than they were. If you had waited for good roads you would have bin here yet. Our wood has bin wet. It couldent get dry from one rain to the next. *[Few things are more miserable than wet wood that sputters along not releasing any heat for drying wet clothes, cooking, etc. Additionally, Nettie is down to her last quarter with only milk and flour for eating!]*

Lyda wasent sick onley the eavening that Add left. She says she is going to write to Papa. We cant all leave at once. Mr. Howell is putting out poisen for the squirrels and we haft to watch the chickens.

Belle, Lizzie, Lyda and I went to Ed Howells yesterday. Lyda walked over there and back. She is trying to jump the rope. Now I want you to write and tell me how you are getting along with the cooking and when you think you can come back. I feal sometimes like I couldent stay here much longer. I would like to see the old covered wagon coming rite now. Tell Clara *[Kellum]* I wish I was over there with her. We are getting along all rite with the work but we dont have enuff to keep us busey, that is what makes the time go so slow.

I sent my other letter to you two weeks ago last Tuesday. It seames like it takes alonge time for the letters to get there. It is 4 weeks to day since you left. What do you do bout bread. Has Clara baked for you yet. Get her to bake when you start back. Wel I must close now. Write soon if you haft to take it to the Office on Sunday.

Mabel will take this to Mr. Hamiltons this morning so they can take it to the P.O.

From S.J.G to Austin

From Austin to Nettie, May 21, 1896

Kamiah
May 21, 1896

Dear Nettie

As Jason is going to town tomorrow I wil try and answer your letters which I received last Monday and was verry glad to hear from you once more. We are all wel. Hope you the same. Wel the sun came up bright and clear this morning for about the first time since we came here and it looks like we might have some better weather.

I am writeing while Add and Uncle is getting breakfast. You wanted to know how we got along with the cooking. We get along all right with that part of it but something to cook is where the trouble comes in. Add does most of the cooking and we get along all right. I guess I would have starved if it hadent been for him. We took some of the East *[Yeast]* and started a sponge and use it instead of butter milk and it makes verry good bread. I wish we had some of the milk and butter you wrote about. We live on bread, a little meat and a few potatoes and watter gravy, and thankful for that. We only make coffee for breakfast. No we aint got Clary to bake any for us till day before yesterday. I got her to bake some light bread to take with me after wheat, but I guess I will have to give up sowing any as we won't have money enough to buy the seed and pay the expenses of another trip out there and back and buy bread to feed us till Uncle get his next pension, and bread we must have. I feel greatly dissipointed about it but I dont know what better to do. I dont think we will have to feed more than 8 or 10 weeks and if we cant get feed in here Uncle says he will take the stock out where feed is cheap and winter them. Wel breakfast is ready so I must quit.

[Austin faced many difficult balancing acts and keeping livestock alive through the first winter was one of those. How could he build a cabin and clear enough ground to raise hay and grain before the first winter? He hints at one solution, take the livestock somewhere else during the winter. The solution they found is not mentioned in these letters and is the reason Woodland received the nickname, "Carrot Ridge". For several winters livestock survived on carrots grown in abundance in the early gardens.]

Wel dinner is over and I wil write some more while the horses rest. I have been hauling logs for the house yesterday and to day. I think I wil get them all in about tomorrow. This is the nicest day we have had since we have been here. The sun is shinning bright and warm. Dumps think they will get their house up this week and then I want to get ourn up as soon as they get theirs done. I tell you Mother I am getting homesick or whatever you are a mind to call it. I laid awake a long time last night and thought of you and the children and of the hardships and difficulties we are going through in our effort to get us a home, but I hope we will be rewarded for our effort in the end. But never mind I am coming after you some of these days if the Lord permits, then we wont be so lonesome.

I would send you some money if I had any way to send it but this aint a Money Order office so I cant send it unless I could get paper money so I could send it in a letter. If you get out of flour before I get back try and borrow some til I get there. I have not heard from Hotchkiss yet. I wrote to him again after we came here.

Add and I went down to the mouth of the Lolo last Sunday. I havent been to Jasons or Dumps except when I had to go for something since we came here and have not eaten at either place. Uncle has been to Jasons a few times. Add aint been to Jasons except on an errand since they came.

Now Maw this letter is for you and not for the neighborhood. We would like to get started back by the first of the month any way but I dont know whether we can or not. Now write as soon as you get this and let me know how you are getting along.

Austin to Nettie

Dear Children -

I ain't got time to write you seperate so I wil write to all at once. Jasons girls says tell you to hurry and come over. Both of their cats got drownded when they upset in the creek. Willie said it was cold in the creek. *[See editor's note below]*

The robbins are singing as hard as they can. There was a couple of big owls in the trees close by last night and they kept up a Hoo Ho about all night. There is a couple of old grouse hens setting just across the creek. It is about time for them to hatch then we will have some little chickens at our house. It looks now like there was going to be lots of goseberries, strawberries and cherries and we saw a good many huckleberrie bushes down toward the Lolo and some of them were in bloom.

Jason brought your letter from the Office last Monday. It came pretty quick dident it. Now see if you cant send another one as quick. Oh yes, Jessie lost his pistol, two knives and a ramrod coming over here and then lost his pony after he got here but it came back. Well I must go to work so good bye.

Father to Mabel, Ora, Stella and Lyda

[When the Kellums (Jason, Clara and family) were moving to their future homestead on "the hill", their wagon upset as they were crossing the creek in Wall Canyon in Woodland. This may have been very close to where the gravel pit is currently located, just west of Steve Tuning's driveway. Flush with the snowmelt, Wall Creek would have been running at or near it's highest seasonal flow rate.

Willie, the youngest, was thrown from the wagon, but he landed on a pillow that kept him afloat until they could rescue him.]

From Nettie to Austin, May 22, 1896

Palouse, Wash.
5/22/96

Dear Austin

I will try to ans your letter I rec'd yesterday. I sent Ora over to Mr. Hamiltons Wed. They said they dident ask for our mail so I got ready yesterday morning, was going to walk to the P.O., went to Mr. Hamiltons but Reg had gone to the P.O. in the eavening and got our mail so I didn't have to go on. When I got back Belle and Lizzie was here. They stayed till this after noon. Lizzie went to town this morning with Hamiltons. She got a letter from Ot's mother and a receipt for their goods, also money order for $8.60. She got it cashed this morning. Ot's mother said Anna Mills was dead at George Sanders. She said she dident know the particulars about her. Said Geo. Kivett was married to Emma Paxton. How is that for high.

I've bin getting in wood and am so trembly that I can't hardly write. We are all well hope you the same. I don't know what is the rip. This is the 4th time I have wrote to you. You said you thought that it was my first. It was my seckond letter and I hadent heard from you at all. You don't like to here from us any better than I do from you. I am so glad the time is getting near for you to come <u>home</u>. It is 5 weeks today since you left. I almost count the hours till you come. We are getting along all rite but we miss you so. If we can't get back when you do come you had better stay and work altho I don't feel like I could stay much longer with out you.

Well the hens have comenced laying again. We got 7 eggs to day, the most we have got for a long time. It has bin like spring the last to or three days till today. It has been cloudy and rained alittle this eavening.

Have you wrote to Jim Hotchkiss yet. Maybe he is waiting to heare from you. No the catalog hasent come here. Lyda is getting so fat you wont know her when you get home. She gets your letters and reads them, you had aught to hear her. Has Add took land and have you kill any deer yet? The children pulled off their shoes yesterday and went in their stockings, their shoes is getting so bad.

Mr. Hamilton is going to take their milk to the Creamery ever day next week so we can heare from the Office ever day. How much wheat did you put in? It is raining and the sun shining. Wel I don't reckon it will be worth while for me to write any more letters, if it is as long in geting there as the others you will be at home before you get it. Maby before you get this.

Lyda said tell Papa she teeter tottered. She said tell Papa Diddy like Papa, said Diddy kiss Papa. We have been to Bells to eat three times since you left. Mr. Jays daughter has a boy. The one that has the stutern man. Mr. Hues sold his big horses for $225.00. I wish we had some to sell if we could get that big a price.

I got a letter from Father. I will send it. Mabel got one from Emma. She rote to Uncle, I will send it. Lizzie wrote to Ot, I will send it. We are just out of writing paper. Wel I must close for this time now. Write soon or better still, come and bring the news. From Nettie to Austin

From Nettie to Austin, May 28, 1896

Palouse, Wash.
May 28/96

Dear Austin,

I will try to write to you this morning. I rec'd your letter yesterday and was glad to hear from you. We are all well, except the cow. She has bin sick. She got out in the north pasture Sunday. I went in the eavening after her but she came up to the gate by the house from the north pasture. She seamed as well as common, gave as much milk as common that night. The next morning she dident give a pint. She wouldent lick salt or drink salt water or eat any thing. It was show day down to town and ever body was gone. In the eavening I sent Mabel to Burt H. He came over and looked at her, said he dident think she was dangerous but done nothing for her. The next morning she wasent any beter so I sent Mabel to Mr. Hamiltons and got him to come. He said maby she had lost her cud. He put a rope in her mouth and made her chew it but it dident help her so I sent Ora to Mr. Davids and got 2 lb. of fat meat and gave her part of it. She is better but doesnt chew her cud yet to amount to anything but she is sweaty of the nose and eats some now and licks salt. She has dried up so I dont know whether I can bring her back or not. I dont think she gave three spoons full of milk last night. I am doing all I know to do to bring her to her milk. It is slim eating without milk. We have a little butter yet. I have bin pretty <u>blue</u> since the cow was sick. I have quite a headache this morning. I never went to sleep till almost 1 o'clock last night.

The little calf got in the N. Pasture with a old bull. We had quite a time getting it out. Yesterday and to day is like spring, it is so nice. The roads are drying up nice here. Wel I am real sorry you can't sow any wheat but we will haft to do the best we can. Well, Belle and Lizzie is here. They came about half past 10 o'clock. Lizzie said to tell you to tell Ot [*her husband*] she guessed she would wait till he came home then she would talk him to death.

Well we will haft to look on the bright side of things and not on the dark. When we get the home fixed up and get plenty of fruit and be together we will forget about the hardships we are going through with. I feal like this was our worst times.

Well I will send Mabel with this to Mr. H. this eavening. They aim to go to town tonight to meet some of their folks. I can get money of Lizzie. Don't worry about us. Does Add furnish part or does he do the cooking for his bord. It is generly about a week from the time you write till I get your letter.

Have you heard from back Home lately. I wrote to Laura rite away, told her to write to me here but havent heard yet. Well I wil close for my head hurts so bad. Wel I reckon it wount be worth while to write any more if you come home the first week of the month. I am going to look for you by the last of next week. Hoping you are well I wil close. Write soon and often. From Nettie to Austin

Editor's Notes

[The following letter from Austin to his parents and family in Kansas marks a watershed moment for the history of Woodland. His description and optimism begin the flood of other family, friends and fellow Quakers from the border area of Kansas and Nebraska.

As the reader learned from reading Edna Ratcliff's memoirs, as many as 25-30 family units (individuals and individual families) moved from the barren plains to lush Woodland. Word spread quickly based on favorable accounts from Austin and the few others (like Kellums) who forged the early trail.

Imagine you were in their shoes and saw the beauty and potential inherent in that virgin country. I would be excited about raising my family there, as I'm sure you would be also.

As usual, I have taken the liberty of doing some minor editing to improve the flow of this letter, mainly adding paragraphs. Perhaps the economy and efficiency of our ancestors are displayed in these cram-packed lengthy letters with virtually no paragraph breaks. Money spent on postage was money well spent when the entire page was utilized.

Austin, however, had beautiful handwriting. Many of the others included in this volume are equally as beautiful and distinct. I fear our generation has lost that skill.

Notice Austin's transition into "King James English" when addressing his mother, Hannah.]

From Austin to Parents, June 10, 1896

Palouse, Wash. June 10th 1896

Dear Parents & Brothers,

Wel I got back to Palouse about noon yesterday & we got your letter last night. We were glad to hear from you again. I found Nettie & the Children well. I only lacked a weak of being gone two months it seemed like a long time to be away from them. But we have had so much rain this spring we were hindered so with our work & the roads were so bad we couldn't git back any sooner. It is verry wet, cool, backward spring all over the West. Lots of rain but no cyclones.

I am taking the Globe Democrat again & I git all of the Cyclone news. I see there was a family by the name of Carey killed in Southern Kan in a Cyclone. Don't know whether they are any of our relation or not. I am glad we are out of the Storm belt, & I wish the rest of you were to.

The longer I am away from Kan. the less I think of it, & the better I like this country. I like the country down where we are going better than here. We have got better timber & grass & I think a better climate if vines & blossoms are any thing to guess by. I guess there wil be hundreds of bushels of wild strawberries down there. The vines & blossoms are very large & look like they would make a heavy crop.

I got our house up but did not get the floor or the door or windows in. I built it of Red Fir. The logs are hewed on the inside. It is 16 x 24 feet.

I got 11 or 12 Acres of ground plowed. We have nearly 3 acres planted in garden & vegatables. If it does wel we wil have plenty I guess. I think we wil have 100 bushels of potatoes.

Enock Kenworthy came back with us & took the train for Spokane this morning. He has a job running the engine in a brick yard. They aim to move down this faul.

No Mother I don't think I said you had better stay there. If I did I did not mean it that way. I thought it would be better for thee & Father to come on the train if you could as it is a long rough trip for old people. But if I couldn't come as I would like I would come as I could. I think you had better come with the boys than to stay there a lone. I think though you wil stand the trip all right as nothing seems to hurt a person out in the mountains.

The main thing is to be careful about the watter, both for yourselves & the horses, as there is lots of Alkali up the Platt, on the Lamie Plains & I think some on Bear River in this State. Watter wil be scarcer in the Faul than when we came. But by making inquiry you can tell how it is a head & you wil have to stop where there is watter whether it is camping time or not.

Get a good 10 gallon keg with a good faucet & wire it on the north side of the wagon & tack a gunny sack over it so you can haul watter when you get where it is bad or scarce. You may have to haul watter for the horses a cross the Desert. You can find out before you leave the Snake River. They were drilling a wel about half way across the desert as we came but I never heard whether they got watter or not.

Don't get any larriett ropes as you cant use them if you do. Get some trace chains & set them up & get the smith to put <u>rings or dees on</u> them. Don't make them over 9 or 10 inches long, rings included. Get the best of heavy harness leather & make straps 1 1/2 inches wide & hobble them. Put loops in them or they wil get worn & come unbuckled. Don't need any swivels in them. Now don't get careless & think they wil stay if part of them are hobbled but never turn a horse loose unles he is hobbled. Get a good cow bell & put on one of the mares if you have any & I don't think you wil have any trouble.

Make thorough inquiry as you go regarding the road, feed & watter ahead so you wil make no mistakes. For if you get on the wrong road you may go a long way before you see any body to tell you any better.

I wil try to give you the route. Go to Kerney. Follow the Platt to North Platt City. Then take up the South Platt to Big Springs then go west over the hills & strike the R.R. again at Chappel & follow it to Cheyene. Then across the Mountains to Larmie City. Leaving the R.R. to the left you will have a steep mountain to go down coming on the Larmie Plains. Be shure your locks *[word used in the horse & wagon days for the brakes]* are safe for if they should break you wil go to the bottom in a jiffy. If there is any trees where you can get them cut one 10 or 12 inches through as about as big as one team can drag to the wagon. Leave the limbs on. Take a log chain & tie the top to the hind axle & drag it top first behind your wagon. This is the safest way you can lock. You cant rough lock as the stone wil cut the chain all to pieces & then you are gone. *["Rough locking" was a system where chains were used to attach the frame under the wagon to the rear wheels to keep them from turning. Essentially the rear wheels would drag instead of turn.]* Now do this whenever it is possible & you wil have no accidents.

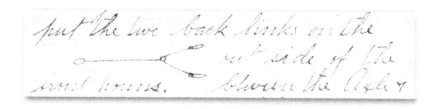

Make your lead bar like this. <u>Put the two back links on the out side of the front horses between the Axle &</u> sand bolsters. Put hard wood keys in the links behind the Axle. This wil save your whealers *[the closest horses to the wheels in a four horse team]* lots as when a wheal drops in a hole or strikes a rock the leaders *[the horses out front]* pull on that wheal which ever wheal is behind thats the one they pull on.

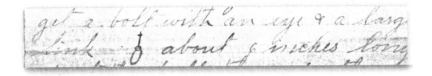

<u>Get a bolt with an eye & a large link about 6 inches long</u>. Put the bolt through the tongue, link down. About two feet & a half from the end. Run the lead bar or chains through the link. This wil let the whealers hold the wagon where you like on curves & let the leaders pull to.

Wel I had better go back to the rout or I will forget where I am. From Larmie City you wil have to go to Saratoga to cross the North Platt River. From there you go North West to Rawlins. From there you go N.W. to Rongis on the Sweet Water River. You follow the Telegraph line all the way so you can't miss the Road from Rongis.

I think it would be best to go by Lander through the Lander Cut off & on to Eagle Rock on Snake River. I think this wil save you nearly a weeks travel & have a better road & feed besides we couldn't come that way in the spring because of high water. But the streams wil be low when you get there. *[Interestingly, Austin advises his parents and brothers to take the Lander Cutoff. Austin and his party took the southerly Sublette Cutoff. The Lander Cutoff climbs at one point to 9,150 feet, making travel in the spring months impossible. We do not know if his parents followed his advice.]*

You wil see freightors between Rawlins & Rongis who can tell you about the road. You must make that a hobby, Inquire, Inquire, Inquire. At Rongis we took up the Sweet Watter to Lewiston from there through the South Pass to Pacific Springs. There you are on top of the Rocky Mountains but you wouldn't know it if somebody dident tell you. There you see the first watter running west tord the Pacific Ocean. From there to Slate Creek Ferry on Green River. Watter wil be scarce between these places & you wil make your Camps according.

From the ferry you follow up Slate Creek to its head where you wil strike another range of mountains. I believe they are called Hams Fork Mts. You pass over these to the West cross Hams Fork Creek (good fish stream) & on west over the mts & strike the R.R. again at Coke Vill on Bear River.

Then follow down the river to Soda Springs (there is where Lorne [their horse] got sick). From there come west down the river about 10 miles till you come to a long snow shed on the R.R. where you turn north. Cross the R.R. at the east end of the shed & strike north west for old Fort Hall in the Blackfoot Indian Reservation. It is about 10 west from there to Blackfoot on the Snake River. At Blackfoot you are at the east side of the desert.

There you wil strike north west for Lost River. Here you wil have 42 miles without watter unless they got watter where they were drilling that well. (Inquire) They were makeing a big irigation ditch about 10 miles west of the river. If they have got it done camp over night at the ditch. Start early & you wil be all right. It is a good road, level & hard.

You wil strike Lost River at an old stage station. Cross the river, go 16 miles S.W. to Arco where you cross the river again. There you start around the Lava Beds for Bellevue on the R.R. From there on west through Cammas Prarie over some more mts & on to Boise City. Here is where you wil see jack rabbits by the thousands.

From Boise N.W. to Emets Ville on the Payette River. Then down the River to Payett where you strike Snake River again. Go on down Snake River to Wieser. From there to Olds Ferry where you cross the Snake River again & then your in Oregon.

From the Ferry go over there to the N.W. 3 or 4 miles to Huntington on Burnt River. Follow up that stream to Baker City & from there to Lagrand in the Grand Round Valley. From Lagrand through the Paradise & Wilough Vallies to Lewiston, Idaho. Then 10 Miles East to Lapaway where you wil strike the road we go to Kamiah. They can tell you there how to get to our settlement.

It is about 150 miles nearer to come from Lagrand to Lewiston than to go by Walla Walla.

If you come by the Lander Cut Off you wil strike the R.R. at Eagle Rock or Idaho Falls as it is called now instead of Black Foot & wil strike the Road we came at Lost River. You must lay in a good supply of grub, feed at Rawlins as you wont strike the R.R. any more til you get to Coke Vill or Eagle Rock which ever way you come.

If there is any thing else you want *[illegible]* just say it & I will tell you the best I can. You wil nead a tent & a stove if Father & Mother comes as the Evenings & Mornings will be cool as soon as you strike the Mts. & you wil nead the Stove to bake bread. I would send you ourn if I could get it to you in time & could get it to the R.R.

If your horses gets poisoned their necks wil cramp like they were choked. Drench them with cold watter. A quart or two.

There wil be no harvest to speak of on the road & it wil be over before you get here. But this *[?]* you can get work plowing *[?]* freighting or something of the kind. A person can get work by taking wheat flour, meat etc for pay when they couldent hire if they had to pay money. I thought such a long trip would be pretty hard on Father & Mother but where there is a wil there is a way.

We saw an old couple down in this state that had come alone from Omaha. They were going to Oregon. The old woman was so crippled up with the rheumatism she had to be helped in & out of the hack & the old man had only one leg. They had the torndownest old rig you ever saw. Their old tub broke down at Boise City & they made up money there & sent them on. The old lady said she was fond of ground hog so I gave them one. So I think if they could make it alone Father & Mother can with your help.

I believe I have answered all of your questions except about the bees. There is some out here. We want to get a start as soon as we can. There is the most & the nicest wild flours over in our country you ever saw but I dont know how much honey there is in them.

Wel I have 7 other letters to answer so I guess I had better quit. We want to start back in a few days. We want to let the horses rest a few days & the roads dry up some. Write to Kamiah.

What was the matter with Annie Mills. We heard she was dead. I read the account of Nute Perrys death in the Globe several days before I got your letter. Wil if you ever got a longer letter than this, good. If you dident send me a Chromo. *[old word for a colored picture!]*

Oh yes, Ad killed a deer about a week before we started home & we are getting fat. We brought some home to Nettie & the girls. Ad came home with me. We are trying to hold down all the land we can for you people. I expect you think I aint going to quit, but I am so good by. Love & best wishes for all.

Austin

Nettie says tell Mother there aint any room for her to write this time. Write soon & tell all the news.

[The following section is uncertain as to date. Most family members feel it was part of the previous letter. However, the paper is much larger, there is a separate signature and it seems to start in mid-sentence as if the first page was missing. Regardless, it contains fascinating information. The first page has a map in the center, see the illustration on page 103.]

If you would like such a place you had better get a russel on you. For I fear it will all be taken up soon. Now we have got a settlement started. I dont know of another such a place any where. It would have been settled up long ago but the Indians claimed it & drove the settlers off. But they cant do it now as the "Res" has been opened for settlement.

You can see by this diagram how we went & where we wil be. The cross south east of Palouse is where we are living now & the dotted line is the way we went. The cross north of Kamiah is where we took land. It is about 125 miles from here.

I broke one of my mules to ride while we were over there. The boys had lots of fun at my expence but I dident get throwed any way. I tried to get Fred to ride him but he wouldent do it.

You must fetch your dogs as there is lots of wolves in the Res. Three came up in about three hundred yards of our camp one morning as we came home but we only had shot guns & they could catch deer in open timber.

Now Mother I wil now try & answer thy questions as Nettie dont feel like writeing she has the head ache. Thee wanted to know if Father could take land. No those who have used this homestead rite cant take land. But the boys can. The land where we are going is not surveyed & may not be for some time. Lora could take a squatters claim & hold it & perhaps he wil be of age by the time it is surveyed. It wont cost us anything til it is surveyed & then only 16 dollars to homestead.

I think that corn wil do all right. I am going to plant what I have of it. How did it do last year. How did the Methodist come out with their racket. Tell us all about it. What are they fussing about any way.

I shot a grouse just a little bit ago & we will have him for supper. Come over. I killed two last evening. Our cow is getting all the grass she can eat & gives a nice lot of milk. We have 12 hens & get 7 & 8 eggs a day. I dont mean that we get 15 eggs in one day but some days get 7 & some days get 8 eggs. They are worth 10cts, Butter 12 1/2 cts. Things are about as cheap over where we are going as they are here.

Good Flour 75 cts per sack, Bacon 10cts per lb., Coffee 25 cts a paper, Shugar 14 lbs for a "$".

I left Cabbage, Tomatoes, & Onion Seed with Enock & he is going to plant them for me. I hope you can sell & come out. It wil take us about all summer to get all of our things moved as it is so far to hall them. Wel I can think of any more to write & I expect you wil get tired before you get this masticated. Write soon & let us know whether you have sold or not. & tell all the news. With love & best wishes for all I am as ever yours.

Austin S. George

Lora you must excuse me for not writing to you individualy as my paper is full & I aint got any more paper till I go to town. You must consider this a pardnership letter ~~when~~ & I wil try & do better next time. I got the largest paper & envelop I could get but they dont hold enough. I expect I wil be at Kamiah when you answer but Nettie can send me your letters & I wil try & answer from there.

Austin's map sent to his parents

Editor's Notes

[The "Lora" referred to is Lorenzo D. George, Austin's youngest brother.

L.D. George homesteaded in Woodland and lived there for the rest of his life. Grandpa John Johnson later purchased the original homestead from L.D. The current owner is cousin Eric Johnson.

Austin's father and mother, Isaac and Hannah, did sell out in Kansas and took the wagon trip with their sons, L.D., Carey and Wilson, in the fall of 1896. Brother Carey returned to Nebraska, for reasons you will learn in a future chapter, and is buried in Guide Rock. Isaac and Hannah lived with L.D. on L.D.'s homestead. They created the first Post Office at that location.

The following letter was written by Austin to Nettie's brother Dave, who lived at the time in Akron, Kansas. The letter was unclaimed and returned.

Dave Haskins later came to Woodland and homesteaded. His choice of property was most certainly dictated by what little remained and he chose the overlooking butte on the north edge of the fledgling community. This summit became known as Haskins Hill, an appellation still used by those who know their history. Dave struggled with the land for a few years and ultimately the property was sold to L.D. L.D.'s family were the owners until May of 2000. In 2015, my brother Jim and I purchased Dave's former homestead.

When I was a wild grandkid running around on the ranch, the property was owned by L.D.'s son, Arden George. Arden and his wife,

Picture on following page: Cabin built by Austin in the spring of 1896. Nettie, Ora and Estella. The child is Minnie Finney. Photo taken around 1912.

Hazel, were two of my favorites. Arden drove the school bus. A bigger man, he always seemed to be cheerful. Possessing a quick easy smile, he liked telling jokes, even to kids like me. Arden farmed with Grandpa Ralph, an informal partnership. When Grandpa Ralph quit haying in the old back-breaking loose fashion, Arden used his new-fangled hay baler to bale the ranch hay. Hazel worked as a school teacher for many years in Kamiah and played the piano at the Woodland Friends Church.]

"Young Freighters". Arden George and Richard Simler (son of Mildred Sanders, Chapter 16).
Hauling groceries for the Woodland Store. Big box in front labeled "Royal Club Coffee"

From Austin to Dave Haskins, October 8, 1896

Kamiah, Idaho
Oct. 8, 1896

Dear Brother and family

After a long long delay I will try and answer your very welcom letter which we received a long time ago but have been so busy have neglected to answer sooner. We are all wel and hope you are all enjoying the same blessing. Fathers ain't got here yet. They stopped a couple of weeks at Boise City and worked and let their teams rest up. We look for them in a week or two.

We have had a very pleasant summer and faul. The nights are quite cool but warm in the day time. Have had some nice rains this faul. The grass is good and wil be till the snow covers it up as the frost dont hurt it.

I dident go out to harvest this year. Uncle went and I stayed to put up hay. I put up 17 loads of hay. I got a letter from Uncle yesterday, the first we heard from him since he left. He said he had stood the work well. He was out of a job when he wrote. He thought he would go out to Walla Walla and look for a job of plowing. Wheat was not as good as last year but the price is about 20 cts better. Everything is cheap here and money scarce but I guess it is the same about everywhere.

Jasen Kellum and I watched a lick about 1/2 mile north west of our house one night about 3 weeks ago and got two nice deer before 11 o'clock. There is plenty of them here but they are so shy they are verry hard to get. There is some bear here to but they are the hardest things to get at you ever saw. It is almost impossible to get them unless we had some good dogs that would tree them. Elwood Ratcliff and John Hodson are here looking for land. The land is being taken up fast, will soon be gone.

Our garden done splended considering it was on sod and put in so late. We will have plenty of potatoes, beets, parsnips, carrots etc. and quite a bit of cabbage. They are working on the Clear Water River dredging out the rapids making a channel for steam boats. We have about 55 little chickens. The hawks have caught several and we have shot several of the hawks. I have got our chicken house done and comenced cutting logs for a stable.

It takes lots of hard work to make a new home in a new country but I think we will be paid in the end. We like to live here. It is so plesant, no storms, cyclones or blizzards. There hasent been a day since we came in here that the wind has blew hard enough to have interfeered with hayeing and when it rains it just comes down strait and easy.

We got a letter from Laury *[Laura, Nettie and Dave's sister]* yesterday sayeing that Emma Haskins had left home. They hadent found her the last we had heard. Dump Ballards will be home tomorrow from harvesting. They have been gone about 9 weeks. Willie George *[Wilbur George, Austin's first cousin]* is up at Palouse and will be here before long.

Wel I must close for this time. This is the third letter I have written this afternoon and have got 2 or 3 more to write. Write as soon as you get this and I wil try and do better next time. With love and best wishes we remain as ever, your brother and sister,

Austin & Nettie to David & Rosy

Editor's Notes

[Finally reunited, the big move from Palouse to Woodland occurred in June of 1896. Together again, Austin and Sarah struggled to build the Woodland farm, clearing timber, adding fields, continuing to improve the log cabin, adding outbuildings, etc.

In the summer of 1897, Austin went to Pullman to work the grain harvest and make extra money as he had done in 1895.

The following letters were written between Austin in Pullman and Nettie, at home in Woodland.]

From Austin to Nettie, August 22, 1897

Pullman, Wash.
Aug 22, 1897

Dear Nettie and Children

As this is another lonesome Sabbath wil write to you again. I am wel and hope you are all the same.

We are having very hot weather out here and the nights are not cool like common. Harvest is verry late this year. We started up and the grain was so green we had to lay off 3 days for the grain to ripen but I got two days work stacking hay so I dident lose it all. The header has bothered some so we have lost some time on that account.

Well I have got my weaks washing done. One shirt, one handkerchief and two pair socks, and am washed and shaved so I feel better. I think this is the last time I wil ever work for a Dutchman. He dont know strait up. Some of the crew are talking of quitting him. Guess I will try and tough it out. He thinks I am all right though. He says I am a good mans.

I hadent had the toothache since I left home until yesterday morning. After breakfast it comenced and just gave me fits. So I was going to try to get some of the boys to work in my place and let me go to town in the afternoon and get it pulled, but as luck would have it the header broke about 7 o'clock in the morning and the boss had to go to town so I went with him and got it pulled. It pulled the easiest of any of them. He got it the first trial. It is 9 miles to town and he drove it in one hour and 7 minutes, and back in one hour and 15 minutes. The roads are awfully dusty here.

Has Enochs *[Kenworthy]* heard from Harley yet. If so where is he. The boys aint comenced work yet. Will comence in the morning. Sherm Hatley and Jeff Stout is working for the Dutchman too. We lost Rock in Pullman. Has Bell heard from Dump and where are they. I wrote to you last Sunday and sent you a dollar in the letter but have got no answer yet. I have made arrangements with the Dutchman to send you 5 dollars next Saturday. Be shure and keep enough for yourself and let Jason have the ballance if there is any.

Write and tell me what all you want me to get while I am here. I don't know whether I will get a chance to send this to the Office right away or not. Write as soon as you get this, as I am anxious to hear how you are getting along. Good bye. Love to all.

Austin

P.S. Have they found Parker yet.

[It is unknown who Parker is, but he is quite a concern and mentioned in several letters.]

From Austin to Nettie, August 31, 1897

Pullman, Wash
Aug 31 97

Dear Nettie and Children

As it rained last night so we couldent work today so I came to town to see if I could hear from you and I got your letter of Aug. 24 and was glad to hear from you at last. I had about concluded that you dident aim to write at all. This is the fourth time I have wrote and only one answer.

Now I want to tell you that I dident send no little slip of paper with Myrtle's things as you say I did and I dont know what you mean about it. I dident know she got any things. *[This little paper caused quit a stir and is mentioned in the letters that follow. Myrtle was undoubtedly Myrtal Kellum, who Wilson George later married. Poor Austin was getting blamed for an evidently flirtatious note authored by Wilson and slipped into Austin's letter. Austin figures it out in the letter dated September 15 that follows.]* No Uncle did not say anything about coming home with me and I did not ask him. He never said anything to me about the $12 dollars and knife he sent Myrtle or nothing of the kind so I dont understand you. I suppose you have got or wil get some more money in a few days as I had some sent to you.

Hatley and the Dutchman has put their crews together and are heading and threshing. They are a daisy outfit shure. We are cutting and threashing at the Dutchmans now and will go to Hatleys in a few days. Myrtle Hatley is helping Mrs. Dutchman cook. Too bad you had such a time after the cow. Who did you trade cows with and did you get a calf with her. It was the understanding when we bought that calf that Enoch was to take care of it till we got back from harvest.

How do you get along for watter. Is it all gone in the pasture yet. How is old July doing, do you hall watter with her. I will write to your father as soon as I can. Write as soon as you get this and tell all the news. Have you had any frost yet. It frosted here the night of the 24th.

I have been about sick for two or three days with the diarhea but am doing some better now. Eat to many apples I guess. Well Ma I guess you will do for a hunter yet. Did the old gun kick? And girls dont you get lost while hunting the cows. How are the squashes and corn getting along? Well good bye for this time. Write soon. Love to all.

Austin

P.S. Tell me all about that slip of paper and Myrtles things.

From Austin to Nettie, September 6, 1897

Pullman, Wash.
Sept 6 97

Dear Nettie and Children

As it has been raining so we cant work and as I am lonesome and nothing else to do I wil write to you again although you owe me two or three letters already. I am well and hope you all the same.

We are working at Mr. Hatleys now. It comenced raining one week ago this evening and has been showering ever since. It rained hard yesterday afternoon and all last night but has broke away this morning. But it will be a day or two yet before we can threash if it dont rain any more. I am afraid I wont get to make as much as I wanted to but wil work as long as I can get anything to do.

How is the corn doing. Do you think we will have enough fead to winter a couple of pigs if I should bring them. I would cut the corn as soon as it wil do as it might get frosted, and the cain to. Is the squash and beans getting ripe yet.

Hal Emery is here working for the old Man. He got here one week ago tomorrow. They have got nearly the whole croud nick-named. They call me Kamiah, another fellow Shorty, another Slim, another Stub, and a man by the name of Sumpter they call Something.

I wish I had got the other wagon fixed and brought it then I could have got a job of halling wheat. It is worth about 70 cts. Do you know what it is worth on the Prairie.

Maud and Nell both have the distemper or something of the kind. Nell is awful poor. I dont know whether she will stand it through or not. This is an awful rough croud and I will be glad when I get away. I guess the Boss will go to town this after noon and I expect a letter from you. It rained on us all the way home from town last Tuesday when I was in and got your letter. We got good and wet.

Have you got that money yet? Has Enochs heard from Harley yet. Wel I can't think of any thing more to write. Oh yes I found a good fruit jar in the field and I picked it up. Worth saving you know. Write soon as you get any of my letters and if you dont get them do as I do. Write anyway. This is the 5th time I have written to you and only got one letter from you. Whats the matter any way. Good bye. Love to all

Austin to Nettie and the Girls

Kiss Lyda for me and tell her I would like to see her and the rest of you.

From Austin to Nettie, September 8, 1897

Wed.
Sep. 8 1897

Dear Nettie and Children

As it is still raining so we cant work I will write a little more. If you get more letters than you want just throw them away. I started you a letter day before yesterday by Mr. Hatley and thought he would get me a letter but it was "Labor Day" and the Post Office was not open so he dident get any. So I borrowed a pony and went to town yesterday and got your letter. Also one from Uncle and one from Clarence Adamson.

I also got some medacine for the horses. I have payed out $1.55 for medacine for them and I dont know whether I will get them through or not. Wel it rained on me all the way home from town last evening and rained all night and is still at it this morning. I fear there wil bee lots of grain spoiled.

I saw Byron Jinkins (a man that worked where I did two years ago) in town yesterday. He took me to the resturant and gave me my dinner. There is lots of hoboes in town. They are drinking and fiting all the time. They have got the jail full and running over. I saw them takeing two men to jail.

Wel I must tell you about the circus we had day before yesterday. While Mr. Hatley was gone to town the boys caught a two year old steer and put the saddle on him and Stub and Slim both road him. He bucked around some but did not do much so they turned him out and run in the big bull and then the fun comenced. They got the saddle on him and Stub bet Hal 50 cts. that he couldent ride him. So Hal went to get on and he never got in the saddle. He just went a rolling so he got up and tried it again. He got on that time but he dident stay half a minute. The bull just sent him a flying. So then Stub thought he could ride him so he tried it and he threw him just as he did Hal and the last time he threw him he struck him on the chin with point of his horn and put a great gash about an inch long and to the bone. So he dident try it any more. Then Slim got on him and the bull gave two or three jumps and stopped and he got off and that ended the show. I laughed till I was almost sick.

Well I am back at the Dutchmans again. We were aiming to hall wheat to day if it hadent rained. I am getting $2.75 a day for myself and 3 horses. When I hired to him I was to put one horse on the header and get $3.00 a day but the horses got sick so I couldn't put them on the header so I had to work for a little less.

Wel I suppose you have got plenty of rain by this time. What did Clarence do with his place. I don't think any of Hatleys wil come back there unless it is Bill. Joe Clawson talks some of going back but I don't think he wil. Now dont worry to hard. There wil be plenty of time to get things done without working day and night. Have you got that money yet. You dident tell me anything about that slip of paper you said I sent and about Myrtles things. I want to know about them.

How is the flour holding out. Dont wait next time till you are in such a hurry before you comence to write as I want to know all about everything. "If Mr. Fox had gone to town what did you want to catch him for." "ha ha" I am glad there was so much wheat. Wish there was as much more. Have you had any ripe mellons yet? I guess I wont answer your Fathers and Careys letters till I get home. You can write to them and tell them I am away from home. Well I cant think of any thing more to write so I wil close. I don't know just when I will get to send this to town but will send it first chance. Good by.

Austin to Nettie & Children

From Austin to Nettie, September 15, 1897

Pullman, Wash.
Sep 15 97

Dear Nettie

As another days work is done and supper over I wil try to answer your verry welcome letter which I received night before last and was verry glad to hear from you again. It seams like a long time between your letters. Wel it has quit raining but I don't know how long it will stay quit.

Wel we have been having a great old time all around. 7 of Mr. Hatleys crew quit him last Sat. Morning. Wils, Lora [Austin's brothers], Wilbur, Shorty, the sack jig, Stub and Slim, so that left him nearly without a crew and the Dutchman quit heading last Saturday night. I went to work for Mr. Hatley and dident loose any time. I made $43 with the Dutchman and will have about 12 days work here and then I dont know what I wil do. Come home if I cant get any more work. The boys are working for a man by the name of Peterson about a mile from here.

I wish I had fixed that other wagon and brought it. I could get lots of wheat halling.

Now about that slip of paper. I was here at Mr. Hatleys when I wrote that letter and as it is Wilson's handwriting he must have slipped it in.

I have been haveing another spell with my bowels but am some better today. I have quit eating anything but bread and gravy and potatoes. I came pretty near sayeing butter but I guess I wont as I aint hardly saw any butter since I left home. I got a box of pills and have took all but 3 and I guess I will take them before I go to bed.

Have you got any more money yet. I told the Dutchman I wanted some money to send to you and he dident have any just then so he said he would borrow it of the Post Master. So we went to see him about it and he said he dident have it to spare just then but would have it in a few days. That was the sat I went and had my tooth pulled I think. I wrote you a letter that day. I think it was the 21st of Aug. He said if I would give him your name he would send you $5.00 the next Sat. That would be the 28th. I asked him about it the last time I was in town and he said he had sent it. If he did send it you should have had it long ago. Now if you havent got it by the time you get this go to the Office yourself and enquire for a registered letter and if you don't get it let me know at once so I can make the Dutchman "dig up" as I dont know what mite happen and I mite want to leave here. I will send you some more money as soon as I can get to go to town.

How is the onions doing, also the turnips and carrots. Don't worry anything about the wheat. When a person does the best they can that is all they can do and it is no use to fret. I hurt my back the other day. I was halling wheat as it is too wet to threash. I never had it hurt much worse. I thought I would be laid up a week or so.

<u>Sept 16</u> and this not gone yet so I will write a little more. We are in the field and waiting for more steam. Had frost night before last and last night to, but is warm in the day. Well we have enough onions to do us. I wish you would see Enoch and get him to write down the number of the Section, Township and Range that we live on and send it to me. I think I know what it is but I must be sure. I will go by Lewiston and see about our land as I go home.

Austin

P.S. Now don't work too hard and get sick. Wel Mother I have thought of what I wanted to ask you. Do you suffer with the cold, the house being so open, and how do you like the cow you got. Paper is full and I must quit. Good By. Do they know anything farther about Parker. Have they arrested Salsberry yet.

Dear Mabel, Ora and Stella -

I will try to answer your verry welcome letters. I was glad to hear you were wel. Wel Mabel I wil try to answer your questions. Myrtle just helped Mr. Dutchman a few days. She dident like the place and dident stay very long. She is here at Mr. Hatleys now. Well Ora Mr. Hatleys have 21 geese and you never heard such a racket as they make sometimes. Wel Stella I sleep out in the barn with the horses and the rest of the hoboes. Oh yes Hal lent his saddle to a boy that was working for Mr. Hatley to go across Snake River week ago Sunday and he dident bring it back so he had to go after it last Sunday. We wil go tomorrow to threash for another man and wil be gone about two days. Wel I am too sleepy and cold to write any more so Good Night. Write soon. This from your Father. P.S. I think it wil frost tonight.

From Austin to Nettie, September 26, 1897

Pullman, Wash.
Sep 26 97

Dear Nettie and children

Your letter of Sep 19th received. I was glad to hear from you once more. I am wel and hope you all are the same. We are haveing fine weather now.

The horses have all got the distemper or something of the kind. It hasent seemed to hurt Maud verry much yet but Fan gave out last Wed noon and Nell last Friday noon so I had to quit work Friday noon. I came up to the Dutchmans that evening. I helped him clean seed wheat yesterday. I will stay here today and help him take some wheat to town tomorrow and get a box to haul the pigs in. If the horses are able to travel Tuesday morning I wil go up about Union town or Genesee and if I can get a job single handed so I can see after the horses and pigs I wil stop and work and if I cant I will go home as soon as I can get there but that wont be very fast. I will have to have help to get up the hill. If I don't get another job you may look for me about Sat or Sunday if the horses don't play clear out. If I get another job I wil write and let you know.

Wel we had another splitup at Hatleys Friday and most of his crew left him. He is a regular old Crank. If I come home I expect I wil get there almost as soon as this letter does but I thought I would write anyway and if I dont get in on time dont get uneasy for I wil have to give the horses lots of time. May have to stop on the road and let them rest a day or two.

I dont know where the boys are as I havent heard from them since they left here. I may get word from them tomorrow. I have a letter for Lora and one for Wilbur. If I dont come home I will send you some money as I dont like to carry it around. I forgot to send you Uncles letter before so I wil send it now.

I would like to have had the numbers of the land before I started home but I think I have them right. Myrtle is still at Hatleys. Joe Clawsons talk of moving over there soon but dont know whether they wil or not. Wel I wil close for this time and wil tell you the rest if I ever get home once more. Yours as ever,

Austin George

Monday and in town. It rained some last night and looks like rain today. I wil start in the morning if it aint raining so I cant.

Austin

Editor's Notes

[Before Austin's death to smallpox in 1908, Nettie and Austin developed blueprints for a proper wood-framed farmhouse. In 1910, Nettie built the house they had dreamed of and planned for. Many neighbors probably helped with construction, but one of the carpenters was Victor Carlborg, whom you will hear from in a later chapter. Victor developed his skills in his father's carpentry shop in Sweden.

Woodland referred to Nettie as "Aunt Nettie", dearly loved, the matriarch of the community. In the fifty-one years after her husband's death, Nettie did whatever it took to scratch out an existence, from farming and ranching to delivering babies as a midwife to raising pigs and beekeeping. Hard times demand diversification, especially when navigating life alone; Nettie never remarried.

A remarkable woman who lived to the age of 94, Nettie passed away about 4 months after I was born. So many years on that wonderful little farm and that is where she died, surrounded by family. And what a family she had. Grandchildren of different generations numbered eighty-four! Yes, she did see me, but at just a few months of age, the memory of the event obviously eludes me. I wish I could have known and remembered her.]

Sarah "Nettie" George

CHAPTER SIX
Wilson George (1872-1951)

Wilson Ragan George

[As you have read, Austin and Nettie's momentous journey and glowing reports of Woodland lured Austin's brothers, his parents and some of Nettie's family, including her dad, John, and brother David. You may have noticed Austin's concerns expressed to Nettie that if his brothers, "the boys" came, nobody would be left in Nebraska to care for Ma and Pa.

The brothers were Lorenzo "Lora", Zenas Carey "Carey" and Wilson

"Wilse". You will now get to meet them in the following chapters. As you can see in the following letter, Wilson was excited about the journey and prospects. His words echo of youth. That time of life when adventure and journey hold the promise of new experiences, stories, and fun. And before the aches and pains mount with old age, when one begins to dread long trips.

Austin and Nettie's families were very intertwined. Carey was married to Nettie's sister, Laura. Austin's sister, Amy Ellen, was married to Nettie's brother, David Haskins. Essentially, three brothers and sisters, of various combinations, married; typical of life in rural America 150 years ago.

Wilson married Myrtal Kellum. They passed away in 1951 and 1952, respectively, and are buried at Woodland.]

From Wilse to Austin, February 26, 1896

No. Branch, Kansas
February 26, 1896

Dear brother & family, I will try to write a little as the rest have wrote some.

We have been hauling hay to day and the hay was so short and the wind blowed so hard we had to borrow sacks to put it in to get it home. We are haveing hot winds now but it isnt damageing the crops much yet except wheat and rye.

About our dogs, I got one, my oldest hound, of a feller south of Burr Oak and she is a flyer. And I have two pups about 6 months old out of the fastest dog in Neb. One is black and the other is blue. They can catch pony rabbits and can help lots in a jack race. I went out yesterday and caught three and caught four Sunday. I am going to make wolf dogs out of the pups, they are sandy now. I caught a wolf the other day.

We went out with the hounds and run across two wolves and I went south and Chess and Carey and some more on the west. And none got on the north and one run out apast me and I got my dogs after him. The old hound caught it and threw it several times and I run up on my pony and shot it with a revolver. I thought she done well for a bitch that had never saw a wolf before. The pups didnt help much but they raised cane with it after it was dead. I didnt have jack along for we was a rabbit hunting.

I have just jumped up and shot at som geese but they was to high. Some of the Widow Busters folks owns the Guide Rock dogs.

Jim Caster is up with his hounds.   Maybe we will go out tomorrow and look for a wolf.

That Wilson you got a letter from is Jessie Wilsons boy.   He said he couldnt come this spring but was comeing this faul. He has hired to Vondy.

Well I guess I have wrote as much as you did so I will quit for this time.   Oh yes Chess has got a Blood Hound.   He is the bigest trailer I ever saw. Write soon.

W. R. G.

Wilson George...hunter

From Wilson to Austin, June 19, 1896

North Branch, Kansas
June 19, 1896

Dear Brother and family -

We received your letter in due time and must say it was an old lunker. We are haveing it awful hot now and it is getting dry too and the grass hoppers and potato bugs are eating everything up. I will be glad when we get on the road.

Solomon Knight *[Solomon's son Allen later came to Woodland and settled]* is here now reading your letter.

Where bouts on your road did you see your antelope? And how many wolves did you see and how close did you get to both of them. I want to know how to practice shooting. I have made some pretty fair shots lately at long range. If I don't get the buck ague I guess we will scare things some. If I can cripple an antelope the hounds will catch him. We havent run the dogs lately. It has been too hot and we dont have any more rain.

We had hot winds some already and the thermometer stands at 96 right now and still going up. We are all going to the river tomorrow to have a swim and fish a little. Careys are going too. The corn is all rolled up and it is up to 100 now but there is a little breeze.

We got a letter from Dave. He said they had a girl and its name is Jessie. We don't know how old it is. Anna Mills *[Harley Hodson's sister]* died with the dropsy. Shiles Kellums has some prospect of selling and if they do they are comeing out there too.

Solomon Knight is talking of comeing on the train in July. If he does don't let him have any land you have staked off for us folks.

Carey don't want to start till after the fourth but the rest of us would like to start by the first. There is lots to do when it comes to get everything ready. We have our (?) made. We made them ourselves, bent the irons and made the holes and all.

Well I will quit and let someone else write. Write as soon as you get this and we will get an answer before we start.

W. R. George
(22 years old)

[Wilson would have been 23 years old at the time of this letter since he was born on September 2, 1872. Did he forget how old he was? The following small note was enclosed with a letter that was dated 1896.]

When we was out hunting the other day I saw a notice stuck up which read as follows:

If any man or womans cow or ox gets into this corn his or her tail shall be cut off as the case may be.

W. G.

Wanted at North Branch Academy a young lady to play a piano with curved legs.

Lost. An old cow belonging to an old woman with brass nobs on her horns.

W. G.

CHAPTER SEVEN
L.D. George (1876-1935)

Lorenzo Dillon George and his wife, Lydia C. Sanders
Children, left to right; Arden, Elsie, Enid, Maude

[Austin's brother Lorenzo Dillon, was known among Woodlandites as "L.D." After arriving in Woodland with his brothers and parents, he homesteaded property adjoining his brother Austin. Austin's efforts to "stake off" a piece for his brother had been successful. Their parents, Isaac and Hannah, lived with L.D. and the first Woodland Post Office was established on that property.

In the letter that follows, dated March 3, 1935, L.D. describes the trip to Idaho to his daughter Enid. Three months after this letter, on June 17, 1935, L.D. died at the young age of 58 in Walla Walla. How fortunate we are that Enid pestered her dad for these remembrances.

L.D.'s wife, Lydia, came to Woodland from North Branch, Kansas in 1902 as a young girl. Her parents, Arthur and Dorcas Sanders rejoined many of their former North Branch friends and neighbors upon their arrival.

I remember Lydia when she lived with her sister Mildred, who was married to my great-uncle Owen Johnson. We will hear from Mildred in a later chapter. Mildred and Lydia also had a brother, Ivan.

Lydia wore her hair much the same as the picture above. A stooped, short, quiet woman, she and her siblings all lived into their nineties. All of the above; L.D., Lydia, Owen, Mildred, Ivan, Arthur and Dorcas are at rest in the Woodland Cemetery.]

From L.D. to Enid, March 3, 1935

Woodland Idaho
March 3 35

Dear Enid

We received your letter of questions Friday but as Sat was Clyde's sale I did not get to answer it until now. We all went to Church today and Mr and Mrs Hoffer came home with us and now Mamma and Arden have gone to church and took them in the little wagon.

Well I will try to tell some of <u>our experiences</u>. We left <u>Kansas July 7th, 1896</u> with one <u>Hack</u>, one <u>two horse wagon</u> and one <u>Four Horse wagon</u> and <u>two</u> <u>extra Horses</u> as ponies. And none to much money for the trip and by the time we got to the Boise Valley we were about out of money and we had lost one horse. All the others were worked down and tired out so we decided we had better stay and get some work and let our horses and mules rest up before we crossed the Mountains to Kamiah.

We were fortunate enough to get a job for the whole bunch of us picking Prunes which we did for about two weeks. It was lucky that we did stop and work as we had to buy at the rate of $40.00 a ton for Hay for our stock before we reached our destination.

When we left Boise we came up a past the Payette Lakes, traveled over Pack Trails that was not built for a wagon road. They were only built for Pack Trains to pack in Provisions and supplies to the mines and there were long stretches where they were what they called Corduroyed where it was swampy and wet.

They built the Corduroy by cutting small trees, cut them in short lengths just as long as they worked the trail wide, which in most cases was not wide enough for a wagon. Consequently we had to let the wheels on one side of the wagons run on the Corduroy and the others off along the side and when those wheels mired down we would pry them up and try it again.

We finally came to the Old State Road [*More info follows at the end of this letter; also see maps on pages 202 and 203.*] that had been built several years before across the Salmon River to old Florence, an old mining town. This road was narrow and in bad shape but was much better than the Trail we had been traveling. The road down on the south side was 10 miles from the top of the hill down to the river and 11 miles from the river to the top on this side. It took us 2 days to get all of our wagons up this hill as we had to put more horses on part of the wagons and leave part of them and then go back and get them. The day we got them all on top it snowed on us most of the day.

We camped at the Salmon River one night and there was an old man lived there in a tent. He was soshing [?] out gold. He had a fine garden which he had raised by irrigating a strip close to his tent. He gave us several vegetables which we sure appreciated as we had not had any for some time. He said he had a family at the town of Clearwater not far from Harpster and when he found out where we were headed for he asked us if we would take what gold he had to his wife. He said she needed it and it would do him no good there. We told him he should not trust it with strangers. That he did not know us or anything about us. But he said he was not afraid to do it and just begged for us to take it but we looked on the map and found it would be quite a bit out of our way to come by his place so we told him we could not come that way as it had been a hard trip already on our horses.

We came on through old Florence an across the flat topped mountain and down to Mt. Idaho, which at that time was the County seat of Idaho County. Then on through Grangeville, down to Stites and Kooskia on where they are now, on to Kamiah, which was the end of the road at that time. From there we just had to put enough horses on a wagon to pull it up over a long point. It took about 10 horses to a wagon and when we got to the top with that one, then we would go back and get another one until we got them all up.

My Brother and a few other families had moved up here in the spring and they helped us to get up the hill. They had raised some gardens but not enough so they could spare much. They did give us some potatoes which we pealed thick and saved the pealings to plant next spring.

The land that was any good had about all been taken. That is as squatter's right. That was all they could do at that time as it is on the Nezperce Reservation and not surveyed at that time.

But there was one fellow that did not want to stay here so he had held a place for us, but there was no house on it. And as soon as we could we commenced to get out logs to build a house of red Fir. We built it 16x24 ft one story high. We cut Red fir blocks for the foundation and set out at each corner where we wanted the house and then in the sides we put in two or three more in line between the two corner ones and then we took the first logs and flattened a place with an axe so they would lay flat in the blocks. Then we cut a place on each in the shape of a house roof. Then we were ready for the first two end logs. On these we cut a V shaped notch to just fit over the end we had shaped on the two side logs. Then we just kept going up until we got up about 8 or 9 ft high then we commenced to form the roof, not with rafters but with

Rib logs.

This is a poor ilustration but you can draw a better one. You see each end log got shorter but the side or rib logs were all the same length. That is they were cut about 2 ft longer than the logs in the walls and they stuck out about one foot on each end so the roof would protect the end of the house.

Then when we got this done we sawed out of the walls a place as wide as we wanted the door. But before we did this we took small poles about as large as my wrist and nailed one on each side close to where we wanted to saw out for the door and windows so as to hold the logs in place until we got the jams nailed to the ends of the logs where we cut them out. The Jamms we made by splitting out slabs about 2 in thick and about 6 or 8 wide. The roof we covered by cutting a big yellow pine tree and cutting off blocks 24" long and then splitting into shakes and nailing to the rib logs. These we put on double so as to break the cracks so they would not leak.

There was a store at Kamiah where we got our nails but that was all we bought as money was scarce, and every thing was high.

I built a fireplace of native rock and Clay in place of mortar and for chimney we split out flat sticks and used clay mud in place of mortar and when I got it built up a foot or so then I plastered it inside to cover the sticks so they would not burn. That way I built it up about 2 ft higher than the top of the roof and as luck would have it I got it so it did not smoke inside the house and drawed fine. And as we did not have money to buy Coal Oil we just done with the light from the fire place.

We had only a sheet Iron Camp stove that we had used on our trip but we had an old fashioned Dutch oven and this we used to bake our bread in the hearth of the Fireplace by raking a pile of Coals out and sitting the oven on them and then taking more and putting on the lid. The lid had a rim around the edges to hold the coals from falling off.

As there was no lumber in the country we made the door out of split shakes. And for hinges we took sticks of stove wood and shaped them like this and nailed one piece to the log and the other on the door with a spike nale through the two ends where the dot is. This made the hinges and for a latch we used a thin piece of fir about 1 1/2" wide and about 3/8" thick by about 10" long, which we call #1. No 2 is catch that No 1 catches behind. No 3 is piece that #1 slides up and down in to hook over #2. No 4 is string that goes through hole in door so you could open door latch and by pulling its string it raises its latch out of the notch #2. No 2 is sloping so when you push the door to the latch raises up and then drops in to the notch holding the door in place.

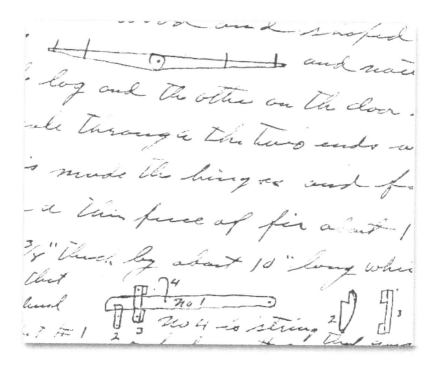

We had no floor for a while only dirt, but one night us boys had been to a spelling school and when we came home and opened the door and stepped in side we went splash and when we lit a match to see there was about 3 or 4 inches of water in the house. There was a place in the corner near the Fire place where the water was coming in so we had to do something so we made a ditch and ran the water out, or all we could, and then the next morning we went and cut some poles and hewed them flat on one side and locked them down and then went and split out some Puncheons [?] flat pieces and took the axe and hewed them as smooth and straight as we could and nailed the ends on the poles and in a few days we had a floor. Not as good as we have had since but none that we have appreciated as much as we did that one.

For Windows we just tacked Flour sacks over the holes we had cut out for the windows. We lived in the house for a few weeks before we made a door. Just had a blanket hung up. After we finished the floor we built a porch the full length of the house on the south by setting posts and then put a pole on top and used other poles from it to the house for rafters and used poles for sheeting to nail the shakes on for roof.

This was during the hard times caused by the wet years of 1893 on for a few years when the farmers lost their crops by so much rain. It was almost as hard to get a job then as it is now but we finally got a job near Kamiah setting fence posts at 2¢ each. There was lots of rock and we did not make much but it was for a Kamiah man and we got enough to buy a sack of Flour. And we killed several deer and so we did not go hungry. This was in the winter and lots of snow.

The next summer or spring we cleared a few acres of land and as there was only one man here at that time who had a plow it was very much in demand and we borrowed it when some one else wasn't using it and finally got one patch plowed and then planted a garden. And what a garden we raised. Well we did not have to go hungry from then on.

As our house was to small we set to work to enlarge it. We built a Kitchen on the west end and by using poles and posts for the frame and shakes for lumber to side it up and to cover it we floored it the same as we did the first part. Then we got along fine for room.

We had brought some carpenter tools and axes with us. For Chairs we split out some slabs about 2" thick and about 12 or 14" square and bored holes in each corner and put in logs.

Quarter to one and am sleepy so good nite. More to follow soon.

With love, Daddy

[Since both this group of hardy travelers and the Hollingsworths, whose account follows in Chapter 13, struggled to reach Woodland on the Old State Road, a short discussion about this route is relevant.

Early in Idaho's history, northern Idaho dominated. The state capitol was at Lewiston and much of the early commercial success in mining was in northern Idaho. Serious wagon travel between the two halves necessitated leaving the state and re-entering, much as the Georges and Ratcliffs did in 1895. The problem was the formidable terrain in Central Idaho, specifically southern Idaho County. Travelers from the south could easily travel up the Weiser River valley to Meadows (also commonly called at the time "Little Salmon Meadows"), but then what? Likewise, travelers from the north found themselves stymied at Slate Creek or slightly further south. The rugged Salmon River and Clearwater River canyons created a natural "line-in-the-sand" for large scale commercial traffic.

In 1864, Idaho's Territorial Legislature convened in Boise having wrested the state capital from Lewiston. Clearly competition between the north and south of Idaho had begun, even as the nation struggled with the division of the Civil War. But early on some legislators felt Idaho would experience more unanimity if an "in-state" road connected the south to the north.

By 1872 recommendations were being made. Eventually, these propositions resolved into two factions. One side wanted the road to go down the Little Salmon River from Meadows to Goff, site of Goff's Ferry. Goff is the current location of the Time Zone Bridge, and this proposed route generally followed the route US 95 follows today.

The opposition proposed the following route: From Meadows up to Payette Lake, following the general route to the mining town of Warren. Before reaching Warren, however, the proposed route would swing to the north and follow French Creek down to the Salmon River. The route would then cross the Salmon river and proceed up the rugged canyon face to Florence. From Florence, the road would follow the Milner Trail across the ridge tops before descending into Mt. Idaho, Idaho County's county seat.

In 1877 the Territorial Legislature passed a memorial resolution requesting the Federal Government for $80,000 to build the segment up the Little Salmon. Other legislative efforts followed, and all efforts waffled between the two proposed routes with absolutely no progress.

In 1889, Idaho's Territorial Legislature passed the Mount Idaho to Little Salmon Meadows Wagon Road Act. Construction was to be financed by $50,000 in 20-year bonds. The state would finance construction but require the counties to continue maintenance. In May of 1890, the U.S. Congress ratified the Mount Idaho to Little Salmon Meadows Wagon Road Act and work commenced. A few months later, in July of 1890, Idaho achieved statehood. Work continued on the road for a few years and as it did, proponents continued to push for the alternate route. Eventually, the route up the Little Salmon, along current US 95, was completed in 1901.

The Mount Idaho to Little Salmon State Wagon Road gradually fell into ruin. Elevation extremes, deep snows in the high elevations, collapse of the bridge in 1902 (more on the bridge in Chapter 13) and the decline of Florence were all contributing factors.

Regarding the elevation extremes, consider the following: In 1872, Colonel De Lacy surveyed much of the area on behalf of the Northern Pacific Railway. He derived the following figures: Elevation of Warrens, 6,030 feet. Elevation at the Wire Bridge on the Salmon River, 2,165 feet. Elevation of Florence, 6,255 feet.

Based on these figures, our hardy travelers descended their wagons 3,865 feet in elevation for 10 miles (using L.D.'s estimates) until they reached the river. After crossing the bridge they climbed straight up over 4,090 feet in elevation for 11 miles before reaching Florence. "Brutal" is an inadequate word!]

From L.D. to Enid, March 4, 1935

Woodland Idaho
March 4 - 35

Dear Enid:
Second edition ~~Volume~~ Page 13

As we were very much in need of a dining table and had no lumber we had to do the next best so we cut some small poles for legs and split out some long shakes and smoothed them as best we could and made a good size table of them.

Next we cut logs for a Barn and built it about the same as the house except when we got up about 8 ft we cut some good size poles and notched in to the two side logs 2 ft apart and then built it on up about 6 ft higher and used the lower part for stable and the upper part for hay. But this was not room enough for hay so we cut some poles about 20 ft long and cut them like Rafters and put them up in parts like rafters, only the lower ends sat on the ground then we took small poles, nailed them for sheeting to nail the shakes on. We made the roof to come down on each side so it was about 6 ft to the eaves. Then we set some posts under the rafters just under the eaves. This was to keep the long rafters from breaking with the weight of the snow. The next winter as we did not get any grain sowed for hay, we had to cut and put up wild grass hay.

By this time there was quite a settlement here and we had to commence to think about school. There was a woman, Lizzie Dillon, that offered to teach in her home. As we had no school district the people who had children had to pay her. But after a year or two we organized a School District and that called for a School House. And the neighbors all got busy cut and Hewed logs and build a good building and used split logs for seats. They used this house for several years until we got a saw mill here, then they built a good frame School House and had boughten seats.

As we wanted some windows by another winter we got Grandpa Kenworthy to make the sash as he was a carpenter and had tools to work with. He made sash for 2 windows for 8 x 10 glass. Then that fall when I went to harvest out in the Palouse country I bought the glass for them. But we used the same old shake door as long as we used the house.

For Social Activities we had old fashion Spelling Bees, Literaries and Parties, and for Recaretion we coasted on home made sleds and went sleigh riding also in home made sleds.

We brought several cooking utensels with us. Among them was 2 old Brass Kettles, one small one about 2 gal and one large one about 7 or 8 gal. These had been brought from Indiana to Kansas by my Father and Mother when Kansas was first settled up.

I think this is enough of this. I don't expect I have answered all your questions but perhaps have more than you will care to use. I wish you would save your paper for us to read after you are through with it there.

Saturday was a beautiful day so sunny and nice. And we all went to Clyde Moons Sale. They have rented their place to Dick Casmerson [?] and are going down where John Moons are or near there. I bought a Hay Rake, the Bob Sleds that Daddy and Ivan made several years ago and which then had sold to Clyde. I also bought a big Black Sow and 8 of the cutest and fattest little white pigs you ever saw. We could not bring the things home Sat. so Arden, Vaden and myself went after them today. Livers had bought 4 Individual Hay horses and Vaden took 4 Horses and we took 4. The Hog Houses was built on skids so I just nailed some Boards over the door of the one our Sow and Pigs were in and put a chain around the ends of the skids and drug it home on the skids.

O Yes I forgot to say that the weather changed and yesterday it snowed some and rained some and last night more and was it nasty today. Snowed more today but melted about as fast as it fell.

More about bringing the stuff home. I used Livers big team to haul my house and Vaden used another of their teams to haul an empty house and Arden put our four on the Bob Sled and as it had an old Hay Rack on we loaded the other two Hog Houses on it and tied the Hay Rake on behind and he brought them home.

Isaac Cowgal George and his wife, Hannah Carey
Children left to right; Austin, Carey, Wilson, Amy, L.D.

We got a Card from Elsie today. Said they got home all OK about 4 o'clock but said they got stuck once over by the George Harvey Place. Bill Phoned up to Grant and told him he had about a weeks work for him painting. Was the reason they went.

We look for them back when he runs out of work again. Grant sure seemed to enjoy himself while here although he worked pretty hard nearly every day. He said farm life was the only life and Tubby thinks so to.

Mamma's cold is lots better and I guess Daddy is some better to. Arden and I are all O.K. Russel has the Pink Eye and Lady has a Glass Eye. We have our Buzz Saw done and tryed it some the other day. But we had bought a 20" saw and it was to small so we sent it back and ordered a 24". It came today. We sent them 1.97 to pay the difference in price of the saws and for Postage and they sent us back a check for $2.71. Said the saws were cheaper now. That is the way I like to deal.

Enough
With Love
Daddy to Enid

❖

CHAPTER EIGHT
Carey George (1867-1954)

Zenas Carey George, circa 1885

[Carey and Laura epitomize a couple at the mercy of competing pulls and tugs. Carey desperately wanted to go west and seek his fortune with the rest of his family. Laura...not so much. Seeing Nebraska as safe and

familiar, she leaves no doubt she was staying put. In a letter to her sister in May of 1896 (before Carey, Wilson, L.D. and their parents head west in the fall), Laura writes words to the effect of, "Nettie I don't want to disappoint you so I will tell you, I ain't coming out there...I will be left alone in this world. I always think the Lord giveth and the Lord taketh away."

Carey, as you will notice in a few chosen letters to follow, looks forward to an adventure and new opportunities. Westward he goes, most likely despite his wife's pleas. Receiving letters from other family members describing Laura's struggles, he returns to Nebraska. So much could be said, but surely those of us who are married have experienced similar moments and muddled through, achieving some type of livable détente.

Détente may have been fragile, even balanced precariously, as can be seen in Laura's last letter.]

Carey and Laura, later in life
Daughters Lillie (left) and Nettie (right)

From Carey to Austin, March 2, 1896

Guide Rock Neb
March 2, 1896

Dear Brother, I will try and answer your welcome letter. Was glad to here from you. Well it is pretty cold to day. I have bin hauling hay but it is to cold to day. I bought 5 tons at $1.25 cts per ton. I haft to hall it about 7 miles. Ben Watt has bin helping me.

I have bin grubing up trees this winter. I bought a tree of E Peaters but I havent cut it and I guess I wont for I have got enoug with out it.

We had a snow about two weaks ago and I went out home and I and the boys and three or four other boys went out hunting. We caught a wolf and five jacks. We had a big race after the wolf. We run him two miles. We run we dident play. We caught it one mile and half west of fathers. I and Wils was about fifteen rods apart and the wolf went between us. Wils run up to it and shot at it with his revolver but he missed it. You never seen wire fences tore down as fast in your life.

Well I will try and finish my letter. Well it snowed and I went out to fathers yesterday and went hunting. We got after a wolf. We run him nearly to Salem. We wer so far from home I and the boys come back but Ches Shagley and three other boys went on. I don't know whether they got it or not but I dont think they did. You ought to have bin with us. We had lots of fun. I am so sore today I cant hardly set down or stand up. Any thing for a little fun. I rode a bout forty miles bare back at that but I got thair just the same.

It is storming to day. It rains a while and snows a while and sleets a while.

Well Laura isent any fatter than she was when you was here. J B T and some of the girls tended meeting some but he didn't take any part.

Will about Hiram, I don't know what he will do with his plase. He is going to tend Hesters plase again this year.

Father H. *[John Haskins his father-in-law]* wanted to rent me the land I tended last year. Now if I could get land any whare else I wouldent tend it. When I get the plase paid for I will do as I please but we have it so near paid I dont want to loose it. Now is that land home stead land whare you are going. If so what does it cost to take a claim. If it is home stead land I think I will have me one if you go down thair in quire a bout the well business. *[Carey worked a side business as a well driller.]* I want to come out thair and I think I will. What is Uncle Abs PO address and the boys.

The libs dident get Jim Watt, he is to orny. The devil has a mortgage on him. I would like to be out thair and have some fun with them wolves.

Well I guess I have told all I know so I will close for this time. Write soon and often for I like to here from you.

from Carey
to Austin and family

From Carey to Austin, April 20, 1896

Guide Rock Neb
April 20, 1896

Dear Brother, as the boys is writeing I will write a little. I am out at fathers to night. I am helping them plow. I am ready to plant as soon as the ground is a little warmer. I will comence this weak if nothing hapens.

Well Ot something is going to drop. I and the boys are coming out thair. We will start a bout the first of July. Can you spare your tent and wagon sheet. If so what will the freight be on them. We will pay freight. Money is hard to get and it is going to take all we can get to get us out thair. We will come with a team. Will you stake of a place for me and do a little work on it. Dont you think that it would keep some one else from bothering it for a while.

Well I took Wils dogs out this after noon and caught a jack. The boys come down to my place Saturday and we went out and run jacks all after noon.

Will I will close for this time. Please write as soon as you get this. from Carey to Ot

Pleas send us the names of the towns you went through going out? Tell us just how you went.

From Carey to Austin, May 31, 1896

Guide Rock Neb
May 31, 1896

Dear brother and sister and girls and boys, as Laura is writing I will write a little. We are all well as comon hope you the same.

Well we had a good rain last night and it is raining this after noon. If we dont get a crop this year it wont be because it hasent rained. Thair has bin lots of storms all a round us. Thair was a cyclone in St Joseph Mo last Wensday night. They said there was a thousand people killed and hadent found all yet.

The boys was down yesterday and we went to town in the after noon. We sold two calfs to Chess Shagley yester day. I have about 65 acers of corn. I have got 45 acers plowed.

Well the chores is dun so I will finish my letter.

Well some son of a B poisened your old Fanny. She had two pups. One of them got a dose to and they sent the other one up to Hirams and I guess it was old Notty Parsons that done it. If it was my dogs I would get even with him. If I had to nock them nots off his head.

Is thair any vacant land clost to your place yet. If thair is stake of a place for me and if any one else goes to take it just tell them to keep of.

Well I will close for this time. Write soon from Carey to Austin and all.

❖

CHAPTER NINE
Laura Haskins (1863-1935)

Laura Haskins and her husband, Carey George, circa 1890

[This chapter represents the other side of the union. Carey is all about hunting and adventure; his wife about surviving. He needs a new gun; Laura undoubtedly thinks one gun is enough.

One hundred and thirty years beyond this letter, male and female

Idahoans continue to have the same conversation. I've heard, more than once, "You already have one gun, why do you need another one?!" My standard answer, based on logic and highly recommended to you the reader is the following. "One screwdriver is never enough. I need screwdrivers of various sizes and types to be able to loosen or tighten every variation of screw. Guns have various uses as well. I need this gun to...", (fill in the blank here with a reasonable argument).

The purpose of this book was to acquaint you, the reader, with the voices of our ancestors. By now you no doubt feel and hear many of those individual personalities. You are getting to know them. For better, for worse...good days and bad days...they were as human as you or I.

Make no assumptions, however, based on a few words. These letters are like windows into their souls, but sometimes our view through the window is but a partial glimpse. Some exhibit more honesty and angst than others. The following letters are a window into harsh difficult days —days of loneliness, depression and raw nerved survival.]

From Laura to Nettie, July 19, 1896

July 19, 1896

Dear Sister and Family

I will try and answer your welcome letter which I got som time ago but have not answered it. I have had so mutch to do trying to get Carey readdy to go out there. He has bin gon most 2 weeks and still lots of work to do yet and on Sundays do not feal like wrighting.

It is most 5 oclock this time before I could make up my mind to write. I have bin at home all day boath Sundays he has bin gone. I cant read or sleep neather one for I have tried it boath Sundays. So you may know how I put in the time.

We have cleaned a 20 acre field sence Carey went a way, took 1 or 2 rows at one time and went all over it. It was in Kansas and you know how Sun flowers grow there. It dident look like the same field it did when we commenced. I had 3 blisters on one hand and went back in a few days and blistered them open a gain and I took the hide off of the other hand with the scythe. And I cut one thumb for about 1 inch to the bone with the corn knife. It doesent seam to heal up for it is on the joint and it opens up ever time I bend my thumb. I thought at first I couldent milk the cows but I haft to milk 3. One dont know what they can do till they try. I come all most fanting I had to ly down and Della *[Della Haskins our first voice.]* faned me.

I will tell you how much money I have got. I have got just 30 cts and I put the horses in a paster and hent got a $1.00 to get them out with but the horses had to have some thing to eat. Carey traded off all of the <u>oats</u> [?] that was standding out so I cant get nothing there but he had to have a <u>Gun</u>. *[Notice this point is capitalized and underlined!]*

Well I guess I can live with out moneys. My butter and Eggs brought me $1.99 cts this week so if nothing happens to the cow and chickens I will make it all wright. I have 50 or 60 old hens and 150 young chickens. Mother *[Nancy Haskins]* has lost most all of her chickens. They intend to start South in about 2 weeks with the Wagon, take the Boys with them. They want me to take care of there things for them. Want me to move down there. There will bee six cows to milk and maby 7 of them besides the other work to do. I dont think there will be much left of me when they get back.

Well this is Monday Eve and I will write som more. I washed today and churned and went down to Pa *[John Haskins]* to doctor our Bill horse. He has the hide off of his neck where the collor rub it and I was fraid the flies would Blow it. The horses is in Mr Foutz paster. Mrs. Foutz has another boy baby.

Anna Watt and Will Edgerton so you have got Watt related to you after all. I ment to say they are married. Lee Parsons is married. You wanted to know what we was a goaying to Cal for I thought we would go out there and work. We boath could work and make somthing instead of that we are getting away with what little we have got saved up. I got Carey $6.65 ct worth out of the store for him before he left.

I thought I would write and tell you for probley you would hear that he started without anything. And I sent 2 qt of lard and a part of Sorgum and 8 or 10 lbs of meat. I sent half. We had 1/2 gal of Plums cooked up, 3 lbs of butter, Bread and cookies.

Flour	100lbs	$1.60
Suggar		1.00
Tea	2 lbs.	30
Coffee	1 lb	20
Rice		25 ct
Beans		25 ct
Bakings Pow	2 lbs	20

Salt.   10 ct

Well I am in hopes he is Enjoying himself while I work for what I have to eat.   I have heard all readdy that he wasent comming back, that he had taken all he had with him.

I helped Ma make her a new dress last week and she wants to mak another one next week.   When I was helping her with her dress I said somthing about her haveing so menny dresses. She said she dident intend to leave anything.   I told her I dident want her to leave me anything.

Ma and Pa and Hiram went to Penny Creek to Camp Meeting and they cam home and <u>Pa Hiram Chas Tom Willie John Has</u> went and was gon 2 Days and 2 nights.

I have made Della 2 new dresses and have got one more to make for her yet. Nettie I do not want you to look for som things when Carey gets there or you will be left.   I would liked to have sent you a dress but had to get for Carey and I dident like to go in debet for one. If Carey gets out there I woush you would do his washing and mending for him.   I would rather pay you than someone else.   He may want to do his own work.   If he dos all right.   I want you to write me a long leter for I want to here from there and how things looks.   They look all right here yet I have had ripe Tomatoes and som of our corn is hard Enough to shell.   I will Quit for fear it will make you sick to read it.   Now write soon and often from One that Loves you.

from your Sister Laura to Sister Nettie and Familey.

I will be so loan som while Father is gone.   I dont feal like I could stand it. To have you all gone.

Good By Pray for Me

From Laura to Nettie, Date Unknown

Well Nettie, you wanted to know if we have parted. No, No, no, not as far as I am conserned and you woulden think we was eather if you had seen him tell me good by. I would rather have him with me than all the land in Idaho but we dident have money enough for all to go. So I stayed. I have bin told since he left, by some one, that thay thought his people would do all thay could to keep him there. I cant help it if he would rather stay with his mother than me.

I will tell you how she survsed us before she left. Thay invited us out to stay all night the night before thay left and we went and she picked her self up and went to Mr Persons and stayed all night. I would com but dident have no Waggon onley what had covers on and things in them.

Well I stayed next day and washed for her and took the carpet up and worked hard but I want you to know that I dident eat a bit of her grub. I got stuff out of Careys waggon to eat and I will bee older than I am now before I gos there agin to stay all night. For get it not.

Now Wiltz he called me a darn fool and a darn bitch. He said the darn bitch wanted to clame every thing. I ask him about it. He denied it but I think he said it just the same. It was about the calves we sold. I want you to know I never got a dollor of it just the same.

The reason I wrote this separate, it was because I dident suppos Ott *[nickname for Austin]* would want to here from me, from what I have herd. And he never has wrot a word to me sence he left. He allway says Dear Brother just as though Carey was all there was here.

You don't know how I feal. If you was here I could talk to you better than I can write.

Nettie, I am trying to live a Christian. I never pray at night but what I pray for you.

John Jefferson Haskins and his wife, Nancy Jane Edgerton, circa 1868
Children left to right; David, Henry, Eliza, Laura; Sarah ("Nettie") held by dad

From Laura to Nettie, September 24, 1896

Dear Sister and Family,

I will try and answer your letter whouch I got and was glad to hear from you and that you was well. I hope this will find you well and enjoying your selves.

I hant hardly able to sit up to night. I have had a sore hand. It look lik a splinter in it. I oponed it and it is on my finger next to my little finger on my right hand. It has bin sore for 9 days and it still runs yet.

I would have written sooner but had so much to do and had no good paper. So I took some of Della tablet. I wanted to write before I went to town. I was a goaying to write Sunday and dident have paper. Della paper was at school.

Well Father went down to see how mother would like it down there. She said she wouldent moove down till she went and seen that part first.

If you think I havent had any thing to do you ort to have bin here and help me. I would get up by day light and some times before and work till 10 or 11 oclock at night. In 5 weeks I caned 70 qt of fruit, 6 gallons of Peach butter and made some jelly and put up 5 gallons of Plum in watter and cooked up 1 gal and have made 23 lbs of butter to sell. That is that much a week. Besides drying peaches I do not know how menny for I havent got them all dryed yet, so I can put them away. My butter and eggs some weeks brings me $2.70 some weeks.

Well I got the horses out of Mr Foutz paster. I soled butter at 7 ct a round to pay for them. I woush you had some of my tomatoes that I cant youse.

When I think of the work I haft to do to morrow it dosent seam like I can do it but I all ways have got it done and I reckond I will again.

Well I will try and write some more. One more days work and it is 9 oclock before I am ready to wright. I haft to bake bread and do part of the mopping on Fridays for I cant do it all and go to town on Satterday and I haft to gether corn on Satterdays.

Well Emma Haskins run off frome home one day this week. *[Emma Jeanett, Laura and Nettie's niece, who would have been about 14 years of age at the time.]* The other children went on to school and she dident go with them but went after wards. The last her mother seen of her she was a goaying towards the school house. When the children came home at night Emma dident come with them or hadent bin to school that day. Hyram came down here to see if she had bin here. I dont know wather they have found her or not. I havent seen any of them. She had slip her clothes out so she ment to go for good.

I got a letter from Carey and he sent me a tie for a birthday present. It is pink silk. I was glad to get it. Showes he has not for gotten me if we are a good ways a part. He said one of the horses had died and some of them played out till thay couldent travel verry fast.

Some of the neighbors said I had better writ for Carey to come back for I look so bad. There has more than one told me I look bad. I lack 5 lbs weighen as much as I did when he left. My hart bothers me the other day. I dident know for a while but what I was a goaying to quit breathing.

I hent writing this to hurry Carey back, for I do not intend for him to read this or hear tell of it, for he knows what the Dr told him and that is enought. He went away with out me asking him to go and I hop he will be willing to come back to me, for I feal like I couldent hardly live with out him. You do not now how I feal or never will till Ott leaves you and goes away with his People. Some times I crye till I feal like I cant stand it any longer. I walk the floor or leave the house. I am offell glad I do not haft to stay here for ever and if I do not get better I dont think it will be menny years. I want to live so I will be readdy to go.

I sent a letter out there for Carey and if you dont get it for him it will be sent back before he gets there. I feel to bad to write any more. So good by for this time. Write soon and often and tell all of the newes from your loving sister and the onley one you have. *[Laura and Nettie had another sister named Eliza. Eliza died in 1886 at the age of 27, a week or so after the birth of her 4th child.]* I would like to see you one an all.

Pray for me
from your sister Laura
to sister Nettie

Butter 8 ct
Eggs 10 ct

From Laura to Austin, September 25, 1896

September 25, 1896

Dear Brother Ott,

I will try and answer your letter whouch I got and was glad to hear from you and that you was well. I hope this will find you well.

I dident intend that for you and dident think a bout you a taken it that way till after the card was gon and then it was to late to be help. I am sorry if I offended you and ask you to forgive me and I hope you will. No you dont know what others have said and I dont suppose you ever will know.

You said for me to write the news. I dont know any for I havent bin away from home to eat but once sence Carey went away and I havent bin off of this place but once in most 6 weeks. Only when I went to town. It will be 2 weeks to morrow sence I was to town. Bill Whites wife has a pair of twin girls and Levey Foland is staying there. It is after 11 oclock so I will quit for this time.

Poor papper, poor pencel and a poor writer that got them. I hope you will excuse poor spelling and all together. Now if you do not want to write as Carey isent here it will be all right withe me for I dont like to write. So I dont write any more than I can help but if you write I will try and answer the best I can.

With the Lord to help us if we never meet in this world. I hope we will boath try and live....we will meet in heaven.

Pray for me

from your sister Laura to Brother Ott
Good By

P.S. I went and pulled and piled my tomatoe vines this eaving. I beleave there was a wagon load of them and grate big tomatoes all most as larg as my dubble fist. I woush you foaks had them if you hent got plenty of tomatoes. I put up 27 qt of them and 24 qrts of peaches. We have had peaches for 4 weeks. There is just a few on one tree yet. Will pick them to morrow. Your letter stayed in the office a week before I got it.

Nettie George with her daughters Estella & Ora, circa 1949

From Laura to Nettie, 1898

[Laura and Nettie's mother died on July 6, 1898. The following letter, written after Nancy's death was also written before the birth of Carey and Laura's daughter, Lillie on the 16th of October.

The stifling summer heat, pregnancy, grief and all of the accompanying emotions set the stage for this letter of frustration.]

1898

Well Nettie, I want to tell you a few things a bout my crying this summer. I felt bad a bout mother going a way and on Satter Day night. After thay went a way Carey wanted me to go to North Branch with him so I got Della and my self readdy to go and John had the team hitched up and drove up readdy to go. And when I got my dress on I asked Carey how I look. He said I looked pretty big. He walked out in the other room and said we will go to bed and begain to strip him self. I dident look any bigger than when he asked me to go. I went to Dave the next day and that was the last.

One Sunday morning he spoak a bout goaying to Ben Watt. Or should he wait till after noon to go. I toald him if he would wait till in the after noon I would go with him. So he wouldent go at tall on Tuesday. After ward he went down there and took supper with them. He hasent asked me how I have felt this summer. And when I cry he never ask what the matter with me and he hent ask me this summer what I wanted when he starts to town or if I want any thing.

My stomache hurts so much I have taken more than one crye. I dont dair to eat any meat or gravy or hardly any thing but bread, butter and potatoes, but what I throw it up. I often set down to and crys. Carey cant blame no one but him self for the way I look, Nettie. I dont cair to live. If I go I hope it will go to *[referring to her unborn baby, daughter Lillie, born on October 16.]* so there ont be nothing left to bother any one.

This spring I thought I would hate to die. Ma dont need no one to see after her now and I think the rest are able to look after them selves. I worked so hard this summer and bin so sick and felt so bad I can hardly walk at all. When I get up in the morning the Lords will, not mine be done, if I go. It is all right, no enjoyment here for me.

[A break here as if she began another letter.]

Well Nettie I do not feal well this summer. I would have written sooner and toald you but I thought it would bother you. It seamed as though I couldent write to you. But I thought it would be better to tell you and then if any thing happened to me it wouldent suspris you so. I dident have much hopes of my self any of the time and now I have less than ever.

Mother is gone. I feal like she went a few months a head so she couldent see me go. I will be sick a bout the 18 of October. The first time it may be 2 weeks sooner. It was just 6 weaks to day from the time she left here till she died. The day she died she said that was the day Carey started for Idaho. It seames like it hasent bin nothing but cry sence thay started a way the 25 of May. *[The day her mom and dad went to south Kansas. See John Haskins' letter to follow.]* It was 2 or 3 o clock that day before I could get the beds maid. I would come in to make them I would cry so I would go out of doors and stay while it would be the same thing over when I came in the house. It seamed like some one was dead. I often cry till I gag. I cant eat hardly any thing. I will throw it up, bread, butter and potatoes is about all I can eat and drink. Coffee with white sugar in it and no cream. I feal pretty week some times.

I hent had help to do but one washing this summer. It seames thay dont care much how I work. Thay may think when it is to late.

to Nettie George

I dont want you to tell Careys mother till a bout the time I am sick for I dont think she car any thing for me. If I do go just think I am better off than I was here where there isent nothing but trubble. May God be with you till we meet again, if we ever do.

Laura to Nettie

[I like to think Laura and Carey eventually enjoyed a happy life and marriage; that absence did make the hearts grow fonder; that somehow, eventually, their marriage strengthened as the years gave them a renewed appreciation of each other.

Following the trip by wagon to Idaho with his parents in the summer of 1896, Carey returned to Nebraska the easy way, via train. His severe case of wanderlust flared up once more in 1899, however. As mentioned in Chapter 1, Carey took another trip to Idaho by covered wagon when he assisted another family with the trip. Laura and her little baby Lillie came on the train and joined them at Woodland. After a visit of a few months in duration, Carey, Laura and Lillie returned to Nebraska by train.

Despite her continual concerns regarding her health, Laura lived to the age of 72, dying in 1935. Carey lived a long life, dying in 1954 at the age of 86. They both are buried in the Maple Grove Cemetery in Guide Rock, Nebraska.

❖

CHAPTER TEN
Isaac George (1832-1915)

Isaac Cowgal George and his wife Hannah Carey

[Grandpa Isaac George most certainly had a few doubts about a covered wagon trip to Idaho in the footsteps of his son Austin when he and his wife were in their 60's. But he did not put a pen to that voice and place those doubts in writing.

He and Hannah "stuck" and remained in the community of Woodland. Not only was he the first postmaster, but he served for a time as Woodland's Justice of the Peace. I currently possess the docket book for the Woodland Justice of the Peace. The calm inherent in a predominately Quaker community explains why most of the pages are blank. Like most of these authors, Isaac and Hannah are interred in the Woodland Cemetery.]

From Isaac to Austin, August 27, 1896

Lost River, Idaho
8/27/1896

Dear Children -

I will try and scribble a few lines to you to let you know how we are getting along. We are getting along all right but slow and are all well as common at present. Lora was taken sick last first day and was pretty sick for 2 or 3 days but is about well again. His hand is about well again.

There is a family by the name of Davis from Nebraska traveling with us since last first day. Was a week ago. Today we camped for dinner on Lost River and the old man Davis and one of his boys and Wils took their guns and went south over the hills to look for deer, and we stayed in camp until 3 o'clock and they did not come in so we hitched up and pulled about three miles and young Davis overtook us and said that they had killed one deer and one bear. So we dumped the things out of one of the wagons and boys went after the meat.

8/28 Camped at noon at Arco on Lost River. We made a dry camp last night on account of getting the meat to camp. They didn't get in until one o'clock this morning. We stayed up and kept a fire to guide them in. The bear we think would weigh from 4 to 5 hundred pounds. One shot done him in. He ran about 50 yards and fell dead. The deer was a 6 spike buck and would weigh about 150 lbs.

We pulled here this morning to get water and taking care of

the meat this afternoon. We fell in with Davises of Montpelior. They are nice and sociable people and he is a holesale hunter and full of fun. They were pulling for Boise City but I think they will go on with us.

Pa and Ma

From Isaac to Austin, September 13, 1896

Boise City, Idaho
9/13/1896

Will Austin I will try and scribble a few lines to you once more to let you know how we are getting along. We are all well at present and are getting along slowly. We lost one of our horses last week. He had been sick nearly every since we started. We had one extra horse so it didn't break our teams but some of them is pretty near played out.

We camped last night a few miles east of Boise City with but little grass and not enough grain in camp to feed one horse but some of the men went to a ranch and got enough oats to feed our teams over today, and by tomorrow morning we won't have enough grub in camp to feed one man. We tried to get to Boise City last night and lay in grub and feed but we couldn't make it. We laid off 2 1/2 days at Soldier and let our teams rest. The boys got a little job of shocking oats close to camp. It took them about one hour and they got a sack of oats for it.

We camped at Castle Rock for dinner one day and the boys went up the mountain and killed a mountain sheep. The man we got the oats of told us we might camp on his ranch and have all the grass our horses could eat so we pulled in this morning and camped. The grass is about knee high and is green and nice. The boys is trying to get some work for a few days to get grub and feed. We are about out of money and if we can't get some work I don't know whether we will get through or not.

Davises is still with us. A man and his wife by the name of Gout fell in with us at Solder and are traveling with us. They are going 15 miles N.W. of Lewiston. There is 19 of us in all.

Pa and Ma

[The following message arrived on a postcard a week and a half later.]

Boise, Idaho
9/23/1896

Well Austin we are stopping here and are picking prunes. We are all working. We get $1.35 per day and get all the fruit we want to use. We are all well and harty and will start on again as soon as we get through here. We have got our horses in pasture close by. Wright *[write]* to Huntington or Lewiston.

I. C. George

❖

CHAPTER ELEVEN
John George (1846-1915)

John Lewis George

[John Lewis George was the youngest brother of Isaac. He heard about his nephew Austin's "expedition" to Idaho, maybe through one of Austin's enticing "come on over and join us" letters.]

From John to Austin, March 3, 1896

Glendora Cal. Mar 3. 1896

Dear Nephew & Family

We often think & speak of you but it is not so easy to make an opportunity to write a letter but as it is raining to day I will take the opportunity to write you.

Has been raining most of the time since 11 oc yesterday & some of the time very hard, is now 2:15 P.M. Have had a very dry winter. No rain to speak of for 5 or 6 weaks & only (I think) 3 or 4 inches all together. The prospect for crops looked slim but we may have rain enough yet to make good crops. It had been warm two or three weeks, turned cooler last friday. Then Sunday night froze up the hydrant so we could not get any water from it in the morning (we had a barrel full however). It always has to turn cooler before it rains here.

I a letter from you dated Sept 29-95 guess it was your last, do not recolect whether I answered it or not, but think I did. You requested us to come up & see you & see the country. Would be very glad to do so if we could, but can not now. But the Lord willing we may do so some time. Milton & I have been talking a little to that end lately but it is only talk & that is very cheap in a sense yet some times does not end so cheaply.

We would have enjoyed the expedition with you over in-to Idaho last Oct, especially if we could have taken some of the Deer & Bear. Milt thought if we really set our selves at it in earnest we might get ready for such a trip in a year from the coming April.

The boys talked some last faul of taking a trip up there but it soon died out & we heard no more of it. We have been thinking a good while of going some where as soon as we could get in a shape so we could. It seems like we can never do any thing here but work by the day or month & can hardly get enough of that to meet our real necesities.

We only have Milton, Orpla, May & Alta at home now. Elva was married Feb 16th to Harry Baker. Burt is living with them & has been with Harry several months. Wilbur is working for the same man yet that he was for last year.

Milt said he mentioned to Harry the other day about going to Washington & he told Milt he had better keep still or he (Harry) would be going north before the time. He was talking of going this spring with the boys. They were planning to go on horse back. Wilbur told them that would be the last way he would go.

We have a place rented for this year, there is 80 acres of it but the cleared land was all rented to another man except about 5 acres that was cleared last year which we have with the house & barn, for $5 per month & pay in clearing at $5 per acre & have the use of what we clear. We have 3 acres cleared & sowed to barley for hay & I guess will get wood enough to last the year.

The timber has been cut off so there is not much but second growth & brush, but it is a bigger job than we thought. Ought to have had $8 or $10 per acre. The owner is a lawyer & if you get even with a lawyer you do well.

Well how are you situated for church prileleges. Have you any United Brethren in that vicinity. Do you & Nettie still belong to the UB Church. We united with it since we came to Glendora & like it very well. I suppose you know there is a division in it. The largest society is distinguished as the Liberals & the smaller as conservatives, to which we belong. The latter seperated from the original church on the ground of receiving or retaining members of secret societies & conforming to the world. In many ways we are quite weak. Only about 15 in number & all poor but the few with the Lord is the Majority.

Bro P.B. Williams of Portland Oreg was with us 10 days inclusive of the holidays of Christmas & New Years. He is a power in the hands of the Lord both in the ministry & in the lecture field of the National Christian Association against secret societies. If you should want a lecture on that subject I could heartily recomend him & wait his convenience. You could probably secure him at quite a reasonable compensation. There was a large congregation for a small place. Came out to hear his lecture & he held quite a good congregation nearly every night.

Will I quit to do chores so will write a little more. Mils went to the PO this P.M. but I did not have this ready to send. He went on over to Harry's after Orpha has been staying with Elva 3 or 4 days. I see May has told you about Elva being sick. She was better this evening, set up some to day. Has had no fever for 2 or 3 days. They live 3 miles west of us. Mils & Orpha were in a hard shower coming home. Did not get much wet.

Is there any government land in that part of Wash or Idaho that is worth settling on, or make a comfortable home & livelyhood. Please write & tell about your trip over into Idaho, what you found there or elsewhere. Milt says tell you we are coming.

Affectionately your Uncle J. L. George & family

[And come to Idaho they did. John and his wife Eliza moved to Woodland in 1898 with many of their children. They are both buried there in the Woodland cemetery. Regarding their children we know at least the following:

Wilbur, as you may have noticed, worked with Austin in some of the harvests away from home at Pullman. He died in 1949 in Lewiston.

Milton was married to Lizzie Sanders in Woodland in 1900. They lived in Woodland for a number of years before moving to Lewiston.

May died at the young age of 22, on the 14th of February in 1908, just a few months before Austin died of smallpox. An educated guess might be that May's life was cut short on the same account. She is buried in the Woodland cemetery.

Alta was married to Levi Craven in 1909 in Woodland. She died in 1972 in Lewiston.

Of special interest is the fact that Wilbur is believed to be the first to file homestead papers on the Johnson ranch. Since many of the letters and memories in this manuscript discuss different aspects of homesteading, some clarification might be helpful. The ensuing summarization involves Brody's (the history lover among the grandchildren) favorite president and mine, Abraham Lincoln.

In 1861, at the beginning of the Civil War, President Lincoln took a number of steps that led to the passage of the Homestead Act on May 20, 1862. Lincoln's intent was clear, revealed in a speech made in Ohio, in February 1861. He said the Homestead Act was "worthy of consideration, and that the wild lands of the country should be distributed so that every man should have the means and opportunity of benefiting his condition."

Lincoln alluded to these principles again on Independence Day in 1861, when he expressed the purpose of government was "to elevate the condition of men; to lift artificial weights from all shoulders; to clear the paths of laudable pursuit for all; to afford all an unfettered start and a fair chance in the race of life." These principles Lincoln espoused applied to all men, including those suffering under the yoke of slavery.

Most of the voices in this manuscript enjoyed the blessings of those words as they were able to carve out their own little farms. Lincoln felt the Homestead Act would allow people to elevate their economic conditions and in so doing, elevate the economic prosperity of the nation.

While the Homestead Act was wildly popular, doing the actual work to obtain title to the property diminished the initial enthusiasm of many, a fact reflected by the numbers. Four million claims were made, but only 1.6 million deeds resulted from the claims. The Homestead Act also resulted in only ten percent of the United States being claimed and settled.

The homestead process involved the following: An initial claim was filed, which cost $18. A maximum of 160 acres could be claimed. The claimant needed to be the head of a household or 21 years of age. After the initial claim, the homesteader was required to reside on the land for five continuous years. Additionally, the homesteader had to build a home, farm the land and make improvements. After the five years were complete, homesteaders were required to travel to their county seat with two neighbors or friends. These witnesses affirmed to the government that the homesteader had fulfilled all the requirements of the Homestead Act. This final action was often called "proving the homestead". After successfully completing all the requirements, the homesteader would receive a deed to the property from the federal government.

Which brings us back to Wilbur George. Something caused Wilbur to default on his homestead plans for the Johnson ranch, so he sold his cabin and improvements to Grandpa John in 1901. Grandpa John then refiled homestead papers, eventually proved up the homestead and received title to the land.

I am compelled to share a few more thoughts on this subject. My family, our family history, is dominated by farmers. Sure there are, as we have seen, a few preachers and a carpenter or two, but almost exclusively our ancestors chosen field of endeavor was farming. As far back as I can trace any branch of our lineage we were dominated by people who made tender green things grow. We are a family with a strong "green thumb".

Never look unkindly on such a pedigree. Farming is a humble yet exceptional profession. A life of nurturing green life and soil, of feeding us and our neighbors, brings us closest to our Designer's original intent. After all, He intended for us to care for His created animals and live in and tend His magnificent garden.

Some of our family, in particular, were gardeners of renown. Grandpa John grew an exceptional variety of plants on the ranch. And I say Grandpa John, but really it was the entire family; seven sons, two daughters and a wife that matched John's ability to work. Nearly every type of fruit, vegetable, berry, nut and grain imaginable flourished under their touch. John was known to gather his excess potatoes from the cellar, load them in burlap sacks, and deliver them with horse and wagon to his neighbors in late winter-early spring, when others were running low on such basic necessities. It was whispered among family members that some of these neighbors might not have survived if not for the generosity of the Johnson family. That is the loftiest expression of a farmer, skilled beyond compare and generous at the highest standards.

Likewise, what other country on earth would take thousands of immigrants, provide a quick path to naturalization and give them 160 acres to "benefit their condition"? President Truman, when speaking in front of a Swedish Pioneer Centennial Celebration on June 4, 1948, made the following comments; "...the mainstream of Swedish migration to our shores consisted of men and women with a deep love of the soil. In the great American West, they saw a chance for a future that was denied them in the Sweden of their day. The America to which these Swedish settlers came was a land that needed the hardy qualities they brought. It was not a land that was particularly softhearted towards newcomers, but everyone believed that each should have a fair chance regardless of his origin. The newcomers quickly learned their way about and soon felt at home. The Homestead Act of 1862 provided them, as well as many other pioneers, with an opportunity to acquire land and establish family farms. To the land-hungry immigrants, the tough prairie sod seemed a golden opportunity and they conquered it by hard work...We are very proud of our citizens of Swedish descent and the part they have played in building up the Middle West."]

John Haskins with his daughter Laura, circa 1880

CHAPTER TWELVE
John Haskins (1838-1918)

John Jefferson Haskins

[Austin and Nettie were just getting settled in Woodland, a few years after their arrival, when Nettie received this letter from her father, John Jefferson Haskins, dated September 29, 1898. The letter brings news of the death of Nettie's mother, Nancy, with all the pain and shock thereof.

The Grim Reaper was a frequent visitor during pioneer days. Fast forward three years from the arrival of this letter and Nettie will lose her eight-year-old daughter, Lydia, to Scarlett Fever. Fast forward another six and a half years to April 1908, and Nettie will lose her husband, Austin, to Smallpox.

How would you or I handle what appeared to be an unending succession of tragedies? Nettie somehow handled it in a way that made her stronger. Instead of collapsing inward, she looked outward and immersed herself in the community and the needs of others.

John's style of writing, seen in the following letter, bares his soul regarding his anguish. Maybe it was the grief, and that stream of consciousness writing I referred to earlier, or just his style, but he uses no periods in the entire letter. I have taken the liberty of inserting them, and some other punctuation where appropriate to help the reader focus on what John is saying.]

From John to Sarah, September 29, 1898

Guide Rock, Sept 29, 1898

Dear Children,
yours of the 14 Recd from Iowa

I have been here about 3 weeks. I hope you are all well. I am not well and Oh how lonesome, you han't any ideah, and the longer the worse. I see from your letter you never got my first so I will try to write you again.

As to your Mothers sickness. 4 years ago while we were in Iowa, she had a hard spell of siattice rheumatism and I dont think she ever saw a well day after that. She took medcine of and on ever since and she was a doctring all last winter.

She had a real bad cough all winter and the 25 of May, the day we started south, she was hardley able to ride in the buggy. I bought a new $85 one to go in and I tryed to get her to go on the cars [train] but she wanted and would go with us so as to be with the cows.

When we got more than half way down she got so bad we stoped at Jases Edgertons 4 1/2 day till she got better and then by the hardest I got her to let us go on and after 2 days her came on the cars. She was there 2 1/2 ds when we got there. I found she was worse again. I went right off and got her some medacine. This was Friday. She seemed better so a Monday we moved home, we onley had to go about 1/2 mi.

The good sisters came in and fixed up the things. I done the most of the house work for a week, she helping some.

She seemed so much better the next Tuesday. We got a girl to work for us and got 3 men to work on the foundation for a house. On Friday she picked stems al off goosberries till 11 oclock. She walked out around the house, came back and sat down in the doore and said she would have to rest.

Pritty soon she ran to the bed and began to make a terable nois and gasp for breath. Our girl called frome the doore for me to come there Quick. We all ran, we was about 60 yards off when we got there. It seemed every breath would be her last. The rheumatism had gon to her heart. We worked with her for about 10 minits before she breathed.

I sent for a Dr. He came at once and said he thought she would get along all right. This night was the onley one but what she rested good. She seemed faint and week all the next day but Sunday she got a good deal better and Monday she was up again and eating harty and wanted me to have the men come to work on the house place. I put her off by saying they was bisey in ther corn again.

Tuesday the same and Wednesday she so insisted on it. I told her all wright, I would. She was up all day spreading out her quilt peaces and looking after some of the things we hadn't unpacked. In PM, 2 of the sisters came and visited till 4 pm. One of them said, Grandma I have faith that you will get well dont you? She said I try to have. The women went away about 4 pm.

Your Ma had been sitting in her stocking feet. She got her shoes, put them on, I buttoned them up. I said, Ma where are you going? She said I dont know and started out of the house. I took her arm and she walked about 30 steps, stoped and looked a round a bit and started back.

When close to the doore, she grunted. I said are you suffering? She said my back ackes. She got to the doore and sat down and said give me a dose of heart medacine. I gave her 5 drops then she said, fan me Quick. I grabed up the fan, droped on my nee and put left arm around her sholder and put my left nee up to her sholder.

As soon as I done this she streatened out resting on my nee and shuddred and became limber. I looked around. Her mouth was open and her lips was blue. I said, Willie Grand Ma is ded. She breathed 3 times very easey and was dead in my arms. She never strugled or made any nois.

I held her till Willie called in some of the neighbores to help carey her to the bed.

Our girl was gon picking goosberies. Wm and I was alone. The rheumatism went to her heart. She died at 4:30 PM the 6 of July.

I got her imbalamed. It cost me $15. She was as natural as life 2 ds later when she was laid away to rest.

I think your Ma intended on going to the home place when she started but saw she couldnt and turned back.

The Day before she Died she sang the song, my days are gliding swiftley by and I a Pilgram and stranger. I tried to help her but couldnt for crying. I thought then she saw the end was nigh. I never hered her sing so clear and sweet in my life.

Nettie, I have written all this letter looking through teers. But she rests now and will till the sweet By and By. I offten go about sundown and sit down by your Ma's head and cry till my head and heart aches and wish I was asleeping by her side. It would be far better for me as I have no home now here. I am onley waiting and seeking a biting [bidding] to come.

If I live I expect to go home about the 15 of October and take a field of labor in S. E. corner of Kan. It is much warmer ther than here.

You said, come out there. It costs so much to travel and I dont suppos I would be satisfied if was there.

I was 4 weeks in Iowa. My Bro Marian hant long for this world. He has catarah of the stomac and vomits about every day. Cant eat but little of anything. He thinks hard of Bro Henry, that he dont write to him. He is now living in Stuart, Iowa.

The folks here are pirtty well. I go up to Highs to morrow. Preach there Sunday at 11 a.m and baptize some 3 PM.

You folks can keep this poorley written letter till some rainey day and when you have time, read it. I hope you will write soon to me at G Rock.

Pray for me
your Father

[After the death of his wife Nancy, even though he mentions in the letter he doubts he would be satisfied in Woodland, John moved from Kansas to Woodland, to be closer to his daughter Nettie. He arrives in time for New Year's dinner with Austin and Nettie in 1900. He built a small store on Austin and Nettie's homestead, just north of their log cabin, and commenced the dual role of storekeeper and preacher.

On October 12, 1904, however, he left Woodland and eventually returned to Kansas to Laura and Carey's farm. He was gored by a bull there in July of 1918 and died a few days later at the age of 80.]

❖

CHAPTER THIRTEEN
Ernest & Alta Hollingsworth (1886-1962) & (1887-1963)

Ernest Ray Hollingsworth, circa 1906

[I have a few early hazy memories of these great-grandparents although I am uncertain of the origin of those memories.

Ernest's trip to Idaho was as adventurous as any of the other stories you have read thus far, especially the segment on the old "State Road", described in Chapter 7, that wound down French Creek, across the Salmon

River near the Scott Ranch and up to Florence. A merciless section of road, if there ever was one even in this day and age. Some parts are nearly inaccessible, except for hikers or possibly an intrepid motorcycle rider.]

My Trip West As I Remember It

By Ernest Hollingsworth

I was twelve years old, when my father and mother, Nathan and Rachel Hollingsworth and eight children: Arthur, Edna, Alma, myself (Ernest), Scottie, Eva, Nora and Ira left Galena, Kansas, April 4, 1899 for Woodland, Idaho. My sister Nellie was born in Idaho.

We left with a covered wagon, a covered hack, four horses and a white pup. I remember we camped the second night on the Neosho River. Each of us older children had our certain jobs to do when we made camp. We didn't bring much besides our personal belongings. One of the most important was a camp stove with an oven. Mother always made biscuits, she could make the best biscuits, and we were always hungry. We also brought a rocking chair, some camp chairs, and a fifteen gallon keg for drinking water and cooking. We found plenty of good water along the way until we got to the desert in Southern Idaho. We thought we could kill our meat along the way, but saw no deer or large game to shoot so we got only rabbits, birds and some fish.

Our pup wouldn't let anything come near our camp. I remember Uncle Zeri Hunt, who came with us a ways to see some of his folks. One day the pup was barking at some strangers coming to our camp, Uncle Zeri hissed him. Father said, "don't, he might bite someone!" Uncle Zeri said, "didn't think they would care if I sharpened up the pup a little."

One of our horses was a good saddle horse but was balky in the harness, that caused us lots of trouble. One morning Artie came to father in a hurry and wanted five dollars. Father wanted to know what for. He explained the farmer near where we were camped wanted a saddle horse and would trade a work horse for our saddle horse, so they traded. Artie said, "let's get out of here before they hitch him up." I think our saddle horse suited them.

I don't think they tried to hitch him up while we were there.

We visited two of my Uncles in Smith County, in Northern part of Kansas, for about two weeks. Uncle Ira Hollingsworth lived at Smith Center, and Uncle Frank Chirchill's lived at Oakley, Kansas. It was sandy country, the wind blew so much it made our faces sore.

We older children walked a lot, it worked off some of our excess energy, but we got pretty tired some times. I remember one day while we were walking I saw a young jack rabbit; we looked for something to throw to kill it with but there was neither a stick or a rock handy. I had in my pocket a sack of marbles my cousin had given me while we were there. I took them out, looked at them, then at the rabbit and decided to try to kill it with the marbles. I hit the rabbit but didn't kill it, the dog chased it on to the railroad track and the section hands tried to hit it with their picks and shovels and nearly knocked the dog off the track, but finally the dog caught it. We went back and looked for the sack of marbles but we couldn't find them. By that time the wagon was so far ahead we had to hurry on and didn't catch up for two or three miles.

[Losing a sack of marbles at the age of 12 in 1899 would have been a tough loss. I played marbles with friends in grade school for hours—playing for "keeps"—trying to win my competitors' favorite "aggies". Such play today is more intellectual. Like grandson Tanner patiently and persistently mastering the Rubik's Cube (in increasingly difficult configurations).]

One evening two angry bulls started fighting near our camp. One had his temper cooled by the other one pushing him over a steep bank into the river.

[Following page photo: Ernest Hollingsworth (right) with his first powered saw.]

I also remembered how bad I wanted to shoot the shotgun. So one day father let me shoot at a rabbit, he told me to be careful how I aimed. I got all set and pulled the trigger, it almost knocked me over. I guess I didn't even aim anyway I didn't kill the rabbit.

The treacherous Platt River worried us. It was about 1/4 mile wide and all sand bars and water, the water being about two or three feet deep in places. It had quick sand where emigrants had lost their teams and wagons. All there was to guide us across was wagon tracks and the sand bars that we could see now and then as we crossed. We hurried as fast as the horses could go, even took the whips to them to keep them going. We were very thankful when we got across safely.

We had to find out about good grass for the horses along the way. We would stop and ask the ranchers what they knew. Sometimes we camped early to let the horses eat. If there wasn't good feed where we camped Saturday night we would get up early Sunday, hitch up and drive tell we found good grass. We usually rested the horses on Sunday, but if we had to travel Sunday we would rest on Monday and we didn't travel when it rained too hard, but didn't stop for just light showers. One evening it was pouring down rain and we were looking for a place to camp. We came to the edge of a small town; a man was standing in front of a very large building motioning for us to drive in, we drove in, unhitched the horses and put them in the sheds outside. There were other emigrants camped there also. It was a real nice place to camp. It sure was a big building, could have been a fair grounds, and was used for the benefit of people.

When we got to the Green River the water was too high, so we had to wait for the river to go down a little before the man would come over to take us across on the ferry. He said it was too dangerous to cross when the water was that high. At Fort Steel near the edge of town we saw a tame antelope. It wouldn't let us get very close. One of the children went up toward it and it jumped right over their heads, and took up the road towards a bridge as fast as it could, then came back panting acting as if it wanted to show us how fast it could run. We saw a posse starting out after some Indians that had run off some of the emigrants horses the night before. We had met some emigrants that had warned us about the Indians running off the horses, so we tied ours at night a few times.

I remember one time Artie and Edna saw a flock of sage hens; he gave the lines to her and told her to drive while he went after the birds, he got all nine of them but he got so far behind we had to wait for him. We traveled with other emigrants at different times along the way which helped for company. There was one family, the Dave Royces, that seemed like our own folks. We almost cried when they had to go a different way.

Coming from Wyoming into Idaho, the only road over the summit was the railroad track. We had to follow it for quite aways and it was very bumpy riding over the ties. We left as soon as the train passed and traveled that way until we came to a meadow where there was lots of grass. We drove off the track and was unhitching the team when the express train came through. We hadn't lost any time getting there either. We were traveling with the Barter's then. They had two wagons with them. Their hound dog chased after the express train and was never seen again.

The next place I remember in Idaho was Soda Springs. Here an old man came to the springs with a cup to drink of the spring water. He said, "it was good for one."

We went from there to Black Foot, Idaho where we had to prepare to cross the desert to Arco. In Black Foot we got more supplies including some hay, grain, and all the water we could carry, as we had to take water with us for the horses.

We were about three days crossing the desert. We traveled sometimes at night while it was cool, as it was to hot to travel during the middle of the day. We had to gather sagebrush to burn for wood. We watched the horses while they ate so they wouldn't go looking for water, as we didn't have enough to give them all they wanted. On the way across the desert we met a freighter, the driver came over to our camp and ask father if he had plenty of water to last us through. Father said that he didn't think he did. The freighter always carried extra water with him on all his trips in case he met emigrants that were short on water. He filled the keg and everything else that would hold water, otherwise we would have been without even a drink for about twenty four hours. The freighters knew of a place or places where they watered their horses, about a mile or two off the road that the emigrants didn't know and had no way of finding.

We got to a ranch about 10:00 a.m., where we bought water for the horses. We didn't dare give them all they wanted to drink at one time, just a pailful at a time until they were satisfied.

From Arco we traveled along the North edge of the desert till we came to Dixie, near there we found a cave with over-hanging rocks where people had carved their names. Some were names of people that were living at Woodland where we were going. Near Arco we saw the Craters of the Moon. The lava rock looked like it had poured all over the hillside. Father told us not to cut across, as we had been doing, because the sharp lava rocks would cut our shoes to pieces.

From there we went to Boise, then traveled over the old State Road all the way to Grangeville. At Payette Lake where we camped, there were some other emigrants there by the name of Fiddlers. They were very friendly people and we were glad to be with them.

We caught some fish in the narrows below the lake in the Payette River. The trout had been upriver to spawn and were going back to the lake. We could see them going down, but they wouldn't bite so we made a seine of some gunny sacks we had with us, by ripping the seams and sewing them together, we used chains on the bottom edge for weights and sticks on top for cords. We also sought some with a triple hook and a chalk line.

An old miner on the Salmon river had a fine patch of spuds. Father ask him if he would sell some, but he said, "no, I planted them to eat and not to sell." But father kept talking about the spuds till he finally ask father if he was out of spuds and father told him we had been out for three days. He started digging and when he had about a pailful father told him that would do us until we got to Grangeville where we could get plenty. He said, "who in hell is digging these spuds." And kept on digging till he had about a half a sack, and he wouldn't take a cent for them. He wanted father to take a gold nugget to Grangeville to his daughter but father was afraid he'd lose it, so he said he thought he would be going out in a few days anyway.

[To the careful reader, the above paragraph seems familiar. L.D. George recounted a similar story to his daughter Enid, undoubtedly involving the same miner. This miner must have lived near the Scott Ranch. The crusty old miner evidently "sized up" some of his visitors, giving them a quick character assessment before determining if they would be dependable in transporting his gold to family. Two more trustworthy families might have been difficult to find. Neither family, however, chose to burden themselves with the extra travel and responsibility involved in carrying and delivering gold.]

We had to cross the Salmon River on a swinging bridge, it was very shaky. Father had all of us walk across first except Arthur and himself who had to do the driving. Father took the hack across then Arthur came with the wagon.

[Crossing the Salmon River at the mouth of French Creek, the State Bridge (also typically described as the "Iron Bridge") was as ill-fated as the State Road. Construction was delayed a year because the iron was mistakenly shipped to Spokane. The span of the bridge was measured incorrectly leading to an under estimate of needed material (iron arrived at the location fifty feet short). Regardless, construction was completed in November of 1892.

Traffic commenced and the bridge quickly proved to be a maintenance nightmare. On March 29th, 1902, a bridge inspector reported to the Idaho County Commissioners on the cost of repairs needed for the bridge. Temporary repairs were authorized and the issue of comprehensive repair tabled (to be decided by the electorate at a future date). Ironically, the Iron Bridge collapsed two days later (March 31) and was never replaced.

The architecture type of the bridge is not well known and only one picture is known to survive. This account by Ernest Hollingsworth would suggest the bridge (or part thereof) was of a cable suspension variety. The Hollingsworths crossed the bridge in July of 1899, three years before the bridge collapse. The condition undoubtedly inspired the caution described above.

Next Page: Only known image of the short lived State Bridge. View is toward the south and French Creek. Photographer J.A. Hanson, courtesy Idaho State Historical Society, 1282.

The Iron Bridge is not to be confused with the Wire Bridge, quite possibly one of the first bridges constructed in the State of Idaho. Located about 5 miles upriver from the Iron Bridge, at the mouth of Wind River (known at the time as Meadow Creek), the Wire Bridge was initially constructed in 1867-68. Greatly used by miners traveling back and forth between the gold towns of Florence and Warrens this bridge also had periodic collapses. In June of 1879, the Wire Bridge collapsed while 25 head of cattle and a horse were crossing. Five of the cows and the horse were lost but most of the cows swam safely to shore. The bridge was rebuilt wider, to 4 feet in width and continued to serve. The last collapse of the Wire Bridge occurred in June of 1894. It was not believed to be rebuilt until 1962 when the U.S. Forest Service built a pack bridge at the location. Again in another ironic twist, the Forest Service nearly had the bridge completed in 1961 before anchor bolts in the rock gave way and the new bridge collapsed.]

The Fiddlers had more horses and could travel a lot faster than we could, they crossed a while before. We were three days going from the Salmon River to Florence. The Salmon River grade was very steep and narrow, the last day at noon the horses were tired and we were hungry so we stopped in the road. Just as we were finishing dinner we heard a noise and looked up and here came Will Fiddler with a four horse team and riding a big sorrel saddle horse. He had us put our teams on the hack and he put his on the wagon. The big saddle horse in the lead and away we went without doing our dishes.

Florence was a mining town and mines were running full at the time. I remember a crew of miners coming in for supper. We came to a place called Adams Camp, an overnight camp ground for travelers, now called Adams Ranger Station. Mr. Adams was a bachelor and lived alone. There was plenty of grass on the meadows for the horses so we rested there a day, then went on to Grangeville.

The Fiddlers were horse traders and also made woven baskets of willow. They had some extra horses also a team of Shetland ponies that looked exactly alike. They hitched them ahead of the four horse team and drove through Grangeville, the ponies pranced along like they were showing off. Some people wanted to buy them but he wouldn't sell them. Our horses were getting awful tired and Mr. Fiddler wanted to give father a team and harness but father said, "no!" then he said he would lend them to us so father borrowed the teams and harness. We took good care of them and later Arthur took them over to Weippe, Idaho where the Fiddlers were living. We parted camp at Grangeville, they going another way to Weippe, and we have seen them many times since then.

From Grangeville we crossed the prairie to the mouth of Cottonwood Creek near Stites then to Stewart (now Kooskia), the lower ferry being out, we had to cross on the upper ferry where the new bridge is now. Then up and over the old Kidder Ridge road (which wasn't much more than a trail) and come by Hollingshead homestead where they were just finishing the roof on their log house. Then over the Ace Bumgardner meadows. Some men had just finished cutting the road out across the Caribel canyon, they said we could get across. Ours was the first wagon to cross that canyon. We camped that night at Arthur Moore, then on to Woodland the next day, August 8, 1899 five days before my thirteenth birthday. We were four months and two days making the trip. Father homesteaded near Harrisburg and it is still in the hands of the family.

[The following two pages are maps that show the route taken in Idaho by the Hollingsworths as well as Isaac and Hannah George and sons (Chapter 7).]

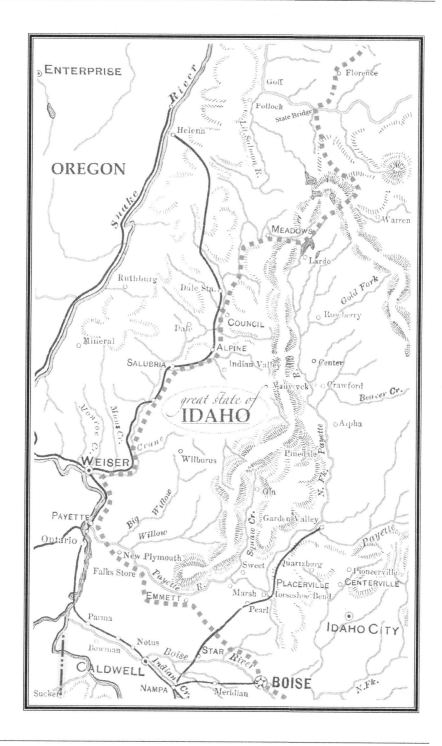

Map labels:

ENTERPRISE

OREGON

River

Snake

Goff

Florence

Pollock

State Bridge

Helena

Warren

MEADOWS

Lardo

Ruthburg

Dale Sta.

Gold Fork

Roseberry

Pafe

COUNCIL

Mineral

ALPINE

Center

SALUBRIA

Indian Valley

Ballyvek

Crawford

Beaver Cr.

great state of
IDAHO

Alpha

Monroe Cr.

Mans Cr.

Crane

Wilburus

Pinedale

WEISER

Oln

PAYETTE

Big

Willow

Garden Valley

Ontario

Willow

New Plymouth

Sweet

Quartzburg

Pioneerville

Falks Store

Payette R.

PLACERVILLE

CENTERVILLE

EMMETT

Marsh

Horseshoe Bend

Parma

Pearl

Notus

Boise

STAR

River

IDAHO CITY

Bowman

CALDWELL

Indian Cr.

N.Fk.

Sucker

NAMPA

Meridian

BOISE

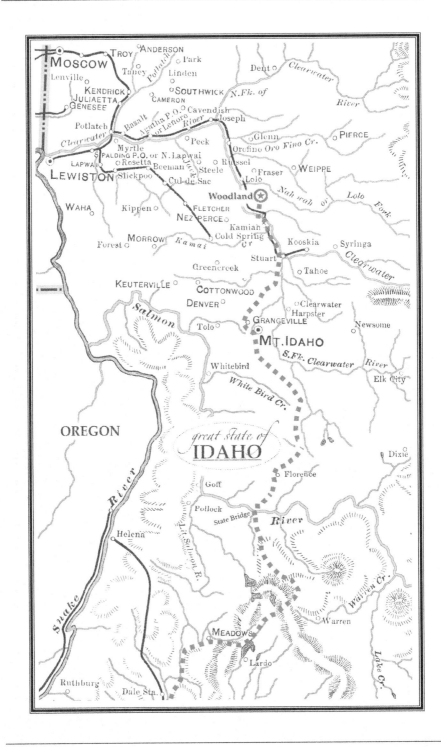

Our Wedding As I Remember It

By Alta "Warner" Hollingsworth

The wedding of Ernest Ray Hollingsworth and Alta Fern Warner, was at the home of the brides parents, Mr and Mrs. Theron Warner, a homestead near Caribel, Idaho April 29, 1908.

The pioneer out-door wedding took place in a lovely grove near the house. The wedding march was played by Mrs. Buell, a cousin of the bride, on the family organ, other appropriate pieces were played on a cylinder record phonograph.

The Rev. J. L. Pearson, of Myrtle, Idaho officiated at the single ring ceremony; the ring placed on the brides finger that day had a rose diamond setting and is being worn by her, fifty years later.

The bride wore white shoes, a grey wool suit skirt, a white silk blouse, with a lace yoke and collar; her flowers were artificial white silk violets she wore in her hair, her jewelery was a pin picture of the groom she wore at the neck of her blouse. The traditional something blue was the blue ribbon that trimed her underskirt, something borrowed was a lace handkerchief of her mothers, which was also something old. Other pieces of her outfit were, a long grey boa stole of Angora; a grey silk blouse and grey shoes that matched her suit, her hat was white trimed with white ribbon, her gloves were white silk.

The brides maid, Eva Hollingsworth, sister of the groom, wore a dress of light medium blue.

[Next page picture: Ernest and Alta departing on their honeymoon, April 28, 1908.]

The groom wore a dark suit and carried a handkerchief of the brides in his coat pocket; Ezra Warner, brother of the bride also wore a dark suit, he was best man.

The table was set for twenty-three and was decorated with Trilliums and other wild flowers.

The brides mother made the wedding cake - which was a fruit cake, she also made the brides cake, which was white, (haveing both cakes was traditional at that time).

Earnest and Beulah Buell had charge of the dinner, the music and took the pictures.

The twenty-five present besides the bride and groom were, Nathan and Rachel Hollingsworth, grooms parents; Al and Edna West and children, (Verla and Earl) sister and family; Alma Ferguson and son George, another sister; Scott, a brother; other sisters were, Eva, Nora and Nellie; Reno and Nettie Hollingsworth and children, (Gladys and Leona); uncle and aunt & family. Theron and Emma Warner, brides parents; Ezra Warner, brother; Earnest and Beulah Buell, cousins; uncle Smith Nethaway and Rev. J. L. Pearson, pastor of the U.B. Church at Harrisburg.

Some of the presents were, cured meat and stored vegetables, N. Hollingsworth and family; canned fruit, Arthur and Bell Hollingsworth, a brother and wife; a brood sow, Al West & family; glass berry set, Alma and family; glass tumblers, Reno and family; white linen table cloth and feather pillows, T. Warner and family; silver water pitcher, Jim and Susie Huddlestone, brides sister & husband, living in Canada; set of cups and saucers; The Buells; two linen towels, Mrs. Myrtle Hurd, a girlfriend living in Michigan.

One of the towels and silver pitcher were exibited at the golden wedding celebration given us, by our children at the Kamiah Grange Hall, April 27, 1958.

Twelve of those present at our wedding are living of which eight...including the brides maid and the best man...were present at the golden wedding.

"Our wedding as I remember it", was writen especially for our children, by their mother, after the golden wedding.

We wish to thank and express our appreciation to our children and their families, for the work and sacrifices it took to give us the wonderful golden wedding celebration, also all those who helped to make the day a pleasant one; and the thoughtful tokens of love given by all. We enjoyed the day so very, very much and will enjoy the memory of it always.

We ask God's blessing upon all,
Ernest and Alta

CHAPTER FOURTEEN
Ray Hodson (1913-2003)

Ray Alfred Hodson

[As previously mentioned, Ray was Grandpa Harold's first cousin and bosom buddy. If the hell they raised as youngsters were recorded, it would make as good a book as any ever penned by Patrick McManus, Mark Twain or Edgar Rice Burroughs. No imagination is needed to see my grandson Blaine cut from the same cloth as these two characters.]

My grandpa Harold Bacon and his BBBF Ray Hodson (right)
Circa 1917

In The Beginning

In 1931 my Dad, Harley and I were part of an elk hunting party that started at Woodland, Idaho. We unloaded the horses along the Lochsa River where we could ford the horses across. The pedestrians rode a swinging basket, two at a time, to the trail head that led us to the top of Coolwater Ridge, overlooking Old Man Lake.

We made camp after dark, too late to set our tent up so we spread our bedroll out on the ground (sleeping bags hadn't been invented yet). When we woke up we were covered with 6 inches of wet snow. It took two days to dry our blankets out.

This trail was completed the previous summer so we had virgin hunting in our area. Our packer was kept busy getting the elk meat into camp, and down to the lockers in Kooskia & Kamiah. He never did get a chance to hunt so I used his 95 Win 30-40 Krag, which is still a good elk rifle (I kept his rifle long enough to drop 3 elk).

Dad and I were hunting together when he dropped a big 5-point bull in a sunny spot so we had to move it into some shade. We weren't equipped for such a job, so I walked about a mile back to camp for a double-bitted axe. On this little side trip I decided we needed two tools - a sharp knife for skinning and a saw for the big bones. I was smart enough to know that I didn't want to carry two such tools, so I figured we wanted one tool that would do two jobs.

The next thing I knew, I was in the Navy. Four years later I was in No. Carolina working for Southern Bell Phone Co. where I was amazed to see a high-speed power hack saw for cutting large pipe, etc. I learned of an old mountaineer that made knives, named Daniel Boone, a descendant of the original. He made me two knives from power hacksaw blades that were 1 5/8" wide and 1/8" thick. The back of the saw blade was sharpened for the knife, cutting edge was 7" long. I know you don't need a hunting knife blade longer than 4" but for sawing through the brisket, leg bone or vertebra of a big bull elk, I wouldn't want a saw shorter than 7". It's good for cutting a meat pole too.

We had a total of 9 hunters in camp, and we brought out 9 elk. That was the "Good Old Days." Roll Call: Geo. Finney, Floyd Finney, Pat Patterson, Roy Emery, Harold Bacon, Harley Hodson, Ray Hodson, Fred Bacon, Carl Peffercorn.

My cousin Harold says the woods are full of those knife-saw combinations now. The steel in the power hacksaw blade makes the best hunting knife I've ever tried. I made the handle and scabbard. The seven little dots and one space is RH in Morse Code ... .

Keep your powder dry and your knife sharp,
Ray Hodson

Tid Bits From My Miss-Spent Youth

First Elk Hunt, 1931, I borrowed a Winchester model '95 .30-40 Krag and Dad had a .303 Sav. that I had killed my first deer with. We packed in on Cool Water Ridge near Old Man Lake on the Lochsa River. Dad & I both got our first elk and both were big 5-point bulls.

There were 7 of us to start with, two more came in a few days later. All 9 filled their tags. We were the first hunting party in that area. All of us except the packer had to walk in. On my 18th hunt I got my 18th elk. Those days are gone forever. I think I went with them, since I was born in 1913.

Later, Al and I were going into camp on the Mud Creek road about midnight when we saw a small bear run across the road. I got a snap shot at it as it disappeared under some tree boughs. Al had the flashlight but it was 90% dead. We ran up to within about 20 ft. of it. Just then the sow reared up on her hind legs over the cub so I took a shot at it and she disappeared. When I extracted the empty, the rifle jammed. I was using a .30-06 Enfield. Next morning we went back but couldn't find the sow or any blood. Anyway we had bear steak for breakfast.

I was deer hunting when I first got my black powder 54 Cal muzzle loader with a set trigger. I use 110 Grs. of black powder and a 410 Gr. slug. I heard a deer coming my way so I sat down, and got ready. But it showed up much lower in the opening that I expected, so I moved the muzzle down and the gun fired before I was ready. I couldn't see anything for the smoke so I sat there cussing myself when I saw a deer foot kicking up over a log. That slug hit just under the deer's skull about an inch. Of course I told everyone I was aiming for a head shot.

I had a Mountain Goat hunt lined up in the near future but I didn't have a rifle that was suitable for that kind of hunting, so I rushed out and bought a .25-06. Everyone knows that you need a long range cartridge for goats. The first morning I spotted a goat working his way up to a high rocky point so I got above him. My long range shot turned out to be 20 yards and I was primed for a 300 yard shot.

More about Bear: Dad was on a forest fire and was sleeping in a tent. The cook laid in a good supply of dried apples and that night a bear came in and had a feast, then went to the creek and filled up on water, but never got out of camp - the apples swelled up and killed it. They didn't even save enough for a pie.

My cousin was working for the Forest Service when he and his partner were sent up to the top of a mountain to start on a new lookout tower and they had to pack the water from a spring. He used two five gallon cans on a pole across his shoulders like the Chinamen do. Harold got up one morning before his partner did so he went for a load of water. When he got back to camp, a bear had his rear end sticking out the open door so he traded his water cans for a four foot limb and sneaked up to his tent door. You guessed it. He broke the limb across Bruin's rump and he went through the tent like a dose of salts. His partner was still sleeping. He and the bear got all tangled up in the tent and they dragged it down the side of the mountain about 100 yards before they could get loose. Harold said his partner never did figure out what happened and "I was afraid to tell him."

Harold Bacon (left) and Ray Hodson
Woodland baseball uniforms on their Grandma Nettie's porch

Bear With .44 Spl On Salmon River

This bear was first spotted while we were moving our Big Horn Sheep hunting camp from Porphyry Ridge (near Chicken Peak) down to the Salmon River. Our pack string was working its way through the timber and brush while Bruin was across the river on an open ridge looking for huckleberries.

We crossed the river on a swinging pack horse bridge.

I didn't want to shoot another bear with my rifle so left it in camp and carried the .44 Spl. S&W with Elmer Keith's big game load of 250 gr. cast bullets. This was a tough hunt. I had to walk at least 100 yards.

He gave me a broad side shot at 35 yds. I thought I overshot as I saw the bullet kick up dirt over his back. He then crossed the creek above me at about the same range and stopped broad side again.

The second shot tumbled him past me at 30 feet. Both slugs went completely through...hide and all...just behind the shoulders... the largest bear I ever tagged.

They hadn't developed the .44 Mag yet.

No, I never got a Big Horn...on this trip. But a few years later I did tag a full curl Dall sheep in Alaska.

The quickest I ever saw a bear give up the fight was with my .54 caliber Muzzle Loader and a 420 grain slug at 20 feet completely through both shoulders. He never grunted, growled or moved a muscle.

Happy hunting and keep your powder dry. Ray

Two Woodland sandlot baseball teams ready for play; don't even try stealing second base! Top photo far right, Harold Bacon; bottom, 2nd from right, Ray Hodson, circa 1920.

A Jump Start

On another trip Emmit Rynearson packed in Harold, Loyd, Dad and myself off the north side of Cool Water Ridge. Dad was the first to get ready for the hike back to the road but he was having some backache so Harold rubbed some liniment on his back and he headed for the road. We thought we would catch up with him at every turn in the trail but we didn't see him until we were all at the truck.

Harold said to Dad, "The way you took off, I thought I must have spread the liniment a little too low."

Ray Hodson

Untitled

A pigeon just flew over and reminded me of another bear story. Bill says he wasn't involved but Clyde, a friend of his, was, so I'll pass it on. I can't "bear" to see it go to waste.

Clyde was poking along a game trail, half asleep when he spotted a half-grown bear coming towards him on the same trail. He wasn't bear hunting, so he stopped to see how close it would come. Finally he got within 5 feet of him and Clyde figured that was enough so he yelled and threw his hat at the bear.

Bruin jumped 3 feet straight up, swapping ends at the same time. When he lit he was in 4-wheel drive. I forgot to mention this was huckleberry season, and the bear didn't have time to close his disposal door. Anyway, I understand Clyde hasn't eaten any huckleberries since then.

Let's go bear hunting, but don't forget your chains.

The moral is: Don't take your hat off in bear country.

Ray Hodson

House Cat or Horned Owl?

In my younger days, we were trying to raise some "drum sticks" for our Sunday dinner, but there was a big horned owl that had the same idea.

One evening, it was almost too dark, when Dad rushed into the house and grabbed the old .303 Savage. We heard him shoot and I went outside and asked if he got it? It was our house cat. When it was silhouetted against the moon, it was the perfect image of a big horned owl on top of the telephone pole.

We got the owl later, before it got any more chickens.

Porcupine Or Coffee Mill?

I was working in Salt Lake City with the A. T. & T. Phone company, when I and two of my buddies decided to go up into the Wind River Range of Wyoming on a fishing trip. My Dad was home at Woodland, Idaho, on vacation, so I invited him to come along.

I hired a packer to take our camp in about 10 miles. Cost all of ten bucks.

In the middle of the first night a strange noise woke me up, that I couldn't identify. It sounded just like an old fashioned hand mill for grinding coffee.

Our phantom coffee fiend was giving the crank a few turns then resting for a spell. I woke Dad up and asked him, "What in the world was that strange noise?" When it was repeated, Dad says, "Porky Pine."

Our packer had packed our groceries in a rawhide pannier and Porky was giving us a duet by chewing on his "drum."

Dad didn't work in the woods all those years without learning how destructive Porky is to anything that has been handled by sweaty hands, such as fishing rods and axes.

My .38 S. & W. ended that problem, I thought.

At this same camp, next day, another Porky came strolling through camp. I started towards it and Porky broke into a trot. I had to shift into second gear to keep up. The first and only time I ever saw or heard of anyone seeing a Porky get in a hurry.

[Following page picture: Estella George & Harley Hodson family. Kids left to right; Faye, Keith, June, Pearl, Ray]

John Cook Ranch

When I was hunting Big Horn Sheep on the Salmon River with Hugh Ellison, we stayed at John Cook's ranch two or three days. I think it was about 13 miles from the end of the road to Cook's ranch. It was on this stretch of trail that we ran into the sow bear with a couple of cubs. She ran her cubs up a tree and we stayed on the trail, or was it the other way around? This is also the area where Cook had an emergency cache in a 50 gallon barrel. The bear couldn't open the barrel so she carried it off and hid it.

John and the Smoke Chaser (SC) were comparing hand guns - the SC had a German Luger, which I noticed was loaded according to the "Loading Indicator." I took the gun and found it to be empty. Later Hugh found the spring on the "Loaded Indicator" was broken.

The Luger had another oddity that could be dangerous. On the side of the action is a metal plate that you remove when you disassemble the gun for cleaning. This metal plate connects the trigger to the firing pin. If I am holding the gun by the pistol grip and passing it to you and you squeeze the metal plate I just mentioned, you will get a hot slug up your shirt sleeve.

Ma, that hurts!

Scared Deer

When I was in my Junior or Senior year in high school, Ezra Warner *[Alta "Warner" Hollingsworth's brother, a great-great uncle of mine. I was honored to serve as a pallbearer at his funeral.]*, Dad, and I were making Cedar poles on Suttler Creek, not far from the Middle Fork of the Clearwater.

We were sleeping in a tent and cooking over an open fire, and waiting for the fire to die down before bed time. Our camp was in the thick timber and it was as dark as it was going to get.

Very faintly we could hear a deer bleating down in the canyon and it was rapidly getting closer. We could hear it running through the brush, and we thought we would see the deer from the light of our campfire. We all had heard stories about a deer that was wounded or scared coming to humans for protection, but our yelling scared it off and it started back down the canyon, bleating at every jump.

I've never heard a more pitiful bleating, which was soon out of hearing.

The Old Timers figured the deer was running from coyotes or a cougar, but we couldn't tell. We hoped it survived.

CHAPTER FIFTEEN
Cora Henderson (1893-1968)

Cora Edna Gertrude Henderson

[Cora was the younger sister of my great-grandfather Lawrence Henderson (Grandma Velma's father).

I don't believe I had the pleasure of meeting Cora, (but would have enjoyed the opportunity). I do remember Grandpa Lawrence and Grandma Ella well. Lawrence seemed a jovial sort with a quick smile. He was definitely a hugger, which is probably where Grandma Velma received her "hugger" genetics. Ella was a small and slender woman, who I've heard was quite a spitfire. I'm sure she smiled, but to me, she was a serious woman and all youngsters are afraid of serious women.

For a time, Lawrence and Ella lived in Woodland and owned the farm where the llama ranch currently is, just east of the Woodland Church. Grandma Velma was around thirteen when her family moved there. At some point following, she and Grandpa Ralph became sweethearts and married.]

Joel Ziba Henderson and his wife, Eliza Elnora Davis, with Vera
Children in back, left to right; Gracie, Cora, my great-grandad Lawrence, Eudora, Lewis

Cora's Life History

The following is the life story of Cora Edna Gertrude Henderson Tilford, written by herself in the spring of 1961.

On Oct. 10, 1893 in Mark, Davis co., Iowa a daughter was born to Mr. and Mrs. J.Z. Henderson. The third child, the oldest a boy Lawrence Leslie and two years later a girl, Grace Mae, two years this the third one.

What should we name the baby? An Aunt was sure it should be Cora, the grandfather equally sure it should be Edna. The mother having named the other girl Grace, knew it must be Gertrude, so poor baby girl was named, not one or two but Cora Edna Gertrude.

But it seemed not too much of a burden to carry, and she grew like other children. Lived in the small town of Mark, where Daddy had a small grocery store. Went to my first term of school to a teacher named Bonnie Bowling. Later daddy traded the store for a farm. I continued to go to the same school. At that time there was one school room and the classes were A. B. C.

A crowded room and one teacher but reading, spelling and arithmetic were taught much as today, along of course with other subjects.

One thrill remembered was my turn to help pass the water. Two pupils carrying a pail of water up the aisles and each child in turn drinking from the same cup, dipped into the pail. No matter if you drank it all, the cup was returned to the pail for the next one. In Iowa the winters were cold with plenty of snow. Many times we walked on a snow drift on top of the fence. Our lunch would be frozen so the poor stove was adorned with lunch pails of all descriptions. The fun we had building snow forts, snow balls and coasting down hill. One time in particular, I remember the Mail Carrier turned in a complaint, we had made the public road so slick he could hardly make the grade.

Life went on in the usual manner, two more children had come to our home. Eudora Faye seven years younger than me (Nov. 3, 1900), then a boy Lewis Wayne, (June 20, 1903), three years younger than she.

In the year of 1904 the farm was sold so the family could go out West. On Mar. 3 our belongings were sold at public auction. Then we were taken the rounds to pay our final visit to the relatives before boarding the train to Lewiston, Idaho. None of we children had been on a train so we were anxious to be on our way. But after having been on the train for three days and nights were equally anxious to get off.

My parents had no money for luxuries so just rode in the chair cars all the way. Poor parents, five kiddies to feed from a lunch basket, and try to find places for them to sleep in a chair car.

Everyone arrived at Lewiston in good shape. We were met at the depot by daddy's second cousin, William P. Henderson and we were taken to his home to stay until we had a place to go. Daddy rented one of his farms which had an old house we could live in. It was a sad looking old house, never had any paint, and well populated with mice. Mother collected news papers and after the mouse holes had been covered with tin, cut from tin cans, the walls were papered with nice clean newspapers. What a scramble was had to find necessary furniture for it. We all had to learn the ways of the west. Had hardships but pleasant new things along with them so all were happy.

How were we children to go to school, two and one-half miles? Walking was in order until the weather got bad, then two saddle horses, we two girls on one and brother on the other. Later we moved to another place and we could walk to school, along with Faye and later Wayne. After we older children got too far advanced for the country school, we were sent to Asotin, Wash. to stay with William Henderson's mother, then a widow. After one year the poor old lady grew tired of keeping us so daddy rented a small house. We batched and went to school. Brother finally quit and Grace and I lived there alone. We were indeed happy and had many good times.

One of our experiences, we always did our school work in the evening at the kitchen table. We had been working and I fell asleep. Suddenly I was awakened by my sister's frightened voice, "Wake up quickly and listen"!! Such a weird sound. She said "bring the lamp into the bedroom and we'll go to bed and put out the light." To no avail, still the weird sound only nearer. We covered our heads and finally fell asleep. In the morning when we dared look out the window, there sat the neighbors old cat. He had gotten locked out of his home and came to our house for refuge.

We had one special girl friend, an only child and a very privileged character, who either stayed at our house or we at her's at least three nights a week. She and my sister were in the same class, so she joined us at the table with school work. One night we were all tired and sleepy and she and I had about fallen to sleep, when my sister called and we looked up to see her in flames. She had a nice new fuzzy outing flannel night gown and had lighted a match and in so doing caught fire on the fuzzy gown. Quickly Eva threw her arms around her neck and proceeded to the bottom of the gown, thus putting out the flames, but not until it had burned the ends of her long hair. It taught us to be more careful with fire.

We were very brave in the day time and at night if we stayed home, but if we went out and had to go in, in the dark, we would ask one of the boy friends to wait until we went inside to be sure nothing was there. Often we were asked if we had looked in the oven or teakettle.

When school was out in the spring we were happy to go home for the summer, but sad too, to leave our friends. In those days there were no cars to drive a distance so it was just good-bye, and hope to see you again.

We had plenty to do at home to keep from getting lonesome. Daddy rented indian land on the reservation at Ft. Lapwai so always took a cook house, as it was too far from home to drive a team. It was my job most of the time to go out and cook for him. The Indians had tepies close and I was desperately afraid of them so stayed in my own quarters when Daddy was out of sight.

In the fall of 1908, we were to have a new addition to our family so the family moved to Asotin for that year. On Oct. 8 a new little daughter was born. How we all adored her. Such a race to see who could hold her, scarcely giving her a chance to sleep. Another burdened little girl. Vera Alberta Blanche. At first she was called Vera, but she grew tired of it and called herself Alberta. After growing up she is now just "Berti" and still adored by the family.

❖

CHAPTER SIXTEEN
Mildred Sanders (1892-1990)

Mildred Ruth Sanders, circa 1917

[Mildred Ruth Sanders was born in 1892 in Northbranch, Kansas. As mentioned previously, she came with her family to Woodland in January of 1902 by train. In the same month, January of 1902, Grandma Hulda Johnson came west on the train, marrying Grandpa John in Lewiston on January 11. So Mildred beat Grandma Hulda to Woodland by a week.

Mildred married Charles Edward Simler in 1917. They had two children, Russell and Richard before tragedy struck the small family. On July 1, 1926, Ed was crushed while working on equipment and died. Mildred was left a widow at 31 years of age.

In 1940, Mildred married my great-uncle Owen Johnson. She was nine years older than Owen. They were married for 42 years until Uncle Owen passed away in 1983.

Mildred and Owen lived in and managed the Woodland Store and Post Office. I liked to visit as often as possible. In fact, one of my earliest memories is of a visit to Uncle Owen's. At the time, we were living in a shack just west of the Woodland School. Around two years of age, I felt the need to be sociable and walked to my Uncle Owen's for a visit. The chat was rudely interrupted by my upset mother. After a frantic search, she had finally discovered my location. The moment engraved its way into my memory, as I received a swat on the bottom every other step all the way home.

Owen's family nickname was "Judge". As the oldest, I guess he served in that capacity more than once among his 8 other siblings. He was reserved, with a quiet voice and manner. Intellectual, with a studious deliberate aura, he subscribed to science magazines and enjoyed conversation about such matters. During one visit he showed me detailed plans he had for building a telescope from scratch, including grinding the lenses!

Owen gifted me with a Swedish book of medical cures and remedies that had been passed down through many generations of Johnson men. Published in Stockholm in 1790, the book still retains a cup shape, presumably formed by the back pockets of numerous ancestors. Owen's signature is in the book on page 100 with the notation, "Woodland Idaho, July 20, 1953", the date of his father's, Grandpa John's, death. The inside cover of the book contains the following notation, (in Swedish, among many other notations), "This book is mine, Johannes Larsson, Hulan". Hulan was the name of the family farm. Johannes Larsson was a distant grandfather. In 2016, I took the book with me to Sweden and signed my name while sitting under a large Elm tree at Hulan. Incidentally, Johannes Larsson was the source of our Johnson name. We are all "sons of Johannes", in Swedish "Johannesson", eventually shortened to "Johnson".

It was easy for me to see how Mildred and Owen ended up together.

Mildred also had a quiet, thoughtful manner, yet she didn't hesitate to set the facts straight if necessary. She possessed a sharp wit that surprised and a quick wry smile that seemingly appeared just when needed.

As you read through Mildred's chapter you will also notice her affinity for animals, seen partly in her recollection of their names. Her photo album is also sprinkled with pictures of horses, dogs, calves, bulls, etc.

My first realization that increasing age usually means increasing the thermostat, or wood stove as the case might be, came from visiting Mildred and Owen. I was amazed at how hot their living space was; the perfect environment for growing the largest Christmas Cactus I've ever seen and for breaking into a sweat within five minutes of arrival. Maybe you, my grandkids, will someday make a similar connection between my age and the inside temperature and declare, "Papa J's finally old now!"

Sanders family
Left to right, adults; L.D. George, Lydia "Sanders" George, Orpah "Ratcliff" Sanders, Ivan Sanders, Ed Simler, Mildred "Sanders" Simler, Dorcas Sanders, Arthur Sanders
Children of L.D. & Lydia, left to right; Elsie, Enid, Maude, Arden

Mildred's Journey West & Early Woodland

Grandchildren have wanted me to write a little about our journey as we started west.

In Dec. 24, 1901 my father, mother, sister Lydia 15, Ivan eleven & myself nine years old, left Aunt Lizzie Kivetts in Jewell County Kansas early in the morning before daylight by wagon for Red cloud Nebraska where we were to take the train for Idaho.

Myrtle Moon (Kenworthy) our Cousin and her husband John Moon & baby Guy about a year old were going with us to Idaho. Uncle Charlie and Aunt Ruth Jones took us by team & wagon to Red Cloud Nebraska with all the freight & luggage we could take on our tickets. Levi took a wagon load too.

Mama had fixed enough lunch to last us for the trip as we could not buy our meals on the train. I think the only hot thing we had, papa had a hot cup of coffee. She fried chicken, made pies, baked bread, cookies etc, enough to last us. We did not take sleepers just tilted the chairs in the cars back & slept. We children did not mind so much but the grown-ups got pretty tired. We were a sorry looking bunch in the morning. We went to the wash room & washed & got our hair combed, then we were ready for our breakfast.

While we were in Montana a very nice looking Indian girl came on to the train, she was wearing beads, beaded headband bracelets & rings. She also wore a beautifully striped blanket, and beaded moccasins. This was very interesting to us children as we had never seen Indians before. She smiled, very friendly. Ivan said "I'm not afraid of that Indian" but he ran down the isle as fast as he could & fell over Papa trying to get to the outside seat.

One night some place in Montana we were to change cars, the trains did not make the right connections & we had to wait most of the night for the train to come that would take us on to Spokane. There was quite a large waiting room and lots of benches & men women & children were sleeping on those benches, finally the train came & we continued our journey on to Spokane.

Mama had an Uncle Joe & Aunt Ann Kenworthy living in Spokane & we went to their house. They had a rather small house nicely furnished, carpets on the floor, over stuffed furniture, plush drapes & dining chairs. This all seemed very great to us, we were used to home made rag carpets & bare floors.

Uncle Will McClure came with a team & hack (spring wagon) & took us to their place about six miles south west of Spokane. We stayed at Uncle Will & Aunt Eslie's for more than a week. They had four children about our ages.

We visited the Whitsons living in Spokane, they were cousins of Mama & Aunt Eslie. They had no children so things were not so intresting (too fancy for me to feel comfortable.)

After about a weeks stay around Spokane we came to Lewiston on the 5th of January., stayed all night at the Grand Hotel which is still standing in Lewiston (1974) but is not a Hotel any more.

On Jan 6 - 1902 we took the train for Kamiah where, Tillie Moon & Elwood Ratcliff met us with a four horse team. Uncle George Sanders also came to meet us on horseback and Grandpa Kenworthy came on Old Minnie.

Elwood Ratcliff had the team they drove west in the late 1880's. *[Small typo or slip of memory there, "late 1890's" as we have read.]* Their names were Lorn & Eagle a dark brown & Lorn was gray. I do not remember Tillie's horses names. I believe it was Tom & Jerry.

We came up the hill after loading our freight and luggage into the wagon. Crossed the river on the Ferry boat very close to where the present road leaves the river & turns north. *[Near the first entrance to the old sawmill site. The first bridge replaced the ferry and the cement piers of which are still visible just upstream near the intersection of Woodland and Glenwood Roads.]* There was not much road we just came over the hills past the old Jimmie Parsons place. When we got up to the road below the Quaking Asp grove we stopped & decided where we would go to spend the night. Uncle George ask us to go there so he got on his little Bay pony, took a trail, short cut right up over the steep hill to tell Aunt Ella we would be there for supper.

We children & Mama had walked quite a lot of the way to make the load lighter for the horses & the men walked all the time.

It was dark when we reached Uncle Georges place.

When we reached Wall Canyon, where the road crosses the creek east of the big tree and the gravel pit, we turned to the right up the bottom of the creek that goes to a field. Uncle Georges house was up in that field about a third of the way up. At that time there was quite large trees there. The field is cleared now & been farmed for many years. There is no sign of the log house Uncle George built or barn or woodshed.

The next morning Jan 7 - 1902 Uncle George brought us to Grandpa Kenworthys. We came from the Hodson place past Elwood Ratcliffs house & to Grandpas place.

We stayed there & we children started to school in the old log school house with Schyler C. Tracey as teacher. I was in the Third Grade. Grandpa Kenworthys' lived in a log house he had built 18 to 20 ft long and 16ft wide (Maybe).

When we came the teacher was boarding with them, he moved to Austin Georges so we could stay at Grandpas.

Papa went right to work building a kitchen for Grandma on the west side of the log house between the house & cellar. He built a cupboard in the wall so milk, cream & food could be passed into the cellar where it was cooler. He also fixed sliding doors to the cupboard.

Papa helped grandpa put in stalls, mangers, floor in the barn & he had a place in the drive-way in the barn where he had his carpenter tools. He built table & three chairs for us.

In Feb he went out toward Grangeville or Stites & bought a team of horses. Bell was gray & weighed about 1400 lbs. Queen was black weighed a little more. We were so very happy & proud of them. Papa always loved a good horse & he took very good care of them. They were the nicest team on the hill.

Papa began to make arrangements to get the place. The man who started to homestead it had left & lived out near Moscow. Also Moscow was the Landoffice at that time.

Papa found Bill Hatley, paid him $100- for his relinquishment on the place & filed for a homestead right.

About this time a man by the name of Bill Bailey claimed he had a right to it. He contested Papas right to file for homestead, and it was seven years before Papa could prove up on the place. This Bailey had never lived on the place or done any work there.

After I went to Moscow & taught school in 1914 & 1915 I paid the attorney who handled the case the last payment $100-.

I should have said Papa made two or three trips with witnesses to Moscow before he could file on the homestead. Then in April we moved from Grandpa Kentworthys down there, into the old log house with the shake kitchen on the east end.

The log part had a half window in the west end with no glass over it. Papa put in a frame & glass. The floor was shakes nailed on to the logs across for sleepers. It was very Rough & some of the shakes were not very smooth. Mama spread straw on the shakes sewed burlap wheat sacks together & made a carpet to cover the straw. It was a very good floor & warmer.

The beds were put in with the heads to the west, one in each corner with a narrow walk way between. Just room enough to make the beds. In the south east corner behind the door was a cot where Ivan slept. Later we had a full sized bed there too. In the shake kitchen was a little window about two feet square with a flour sack tacked on to let in light & keep out bugs. Papa soon cut out for a full sized window and put it in. The floor in the kitchen was shake also, but after a time there was more lumber available so he bought lumber and put new floor in the kitchen. Put in a good door with a pull string latch (neat too). We later had better floor in the log part.

In a few years I think it must have been about 1904 - Papa built a little box stile house on the south side of the old house & put a door in the South West corner of the kitchen to go into the new part. It had a stove in there & was used for a living room (now days a family room). We also used it for we girls bedroom. We tho't we had lots of room but really we were crowded. This was the room where Noan [*Another nickname for L. D. George*] & Lydia were married. Later when we built the big house on the hill, we moved this new part up there & it was used as a chicken house.

Papa built a barn to shelter the team of horses and two cows. They were our source of living and must be cared for. Mama sold butter to the mills later, but at first we sold some milk for making cheese at Grandpas. We also sold garden stuff to the mills too.

Some of the earlier settlers put out strawberry plants that were bearing & they would let us pick berries on the shares. Mama would take Lydia, Ivan & myself & we would pick strawberries till chore time & go home bearing our share of the berries.

We spent a great deal of time at Grandpas that first summer. They were milking cows, making cheese & raising garden & feed for their cows & they needed lots of help.

We cleared more land & seeded some for hay.

Levi & his brother Lineus came from Kansas & stayed with us part of the first winter. We were quite crowded in the old shack but I never heard Mama complain. We were warm & had plenty to eat. Lineus did not stay a year. He had left a girl behind in Kansas & he had to go back. He was married soon after going back.

After the hayshed and barn were built for the horses & cows Papa built a cellar and milk house to store our winter food in & we had the cream separator in here also. It was insulated with saw dust and was cool in the summer & kept the fruit from freezing in the winter.

All the while he was doing the improvements he was clearing land for farming. He built a road from the south forty cut the trees into saw logs & hauled them to the saw mill. This lumber was to be used to build us a house. He made a logging sled with the help of a neighborhood black smith to haul the logs in the winter when the snow was on the ground. The timber was good pine trees. He traded logs for the lumber. He must have hauled them two miles or more to the saw mill so it was a long tedious job. Some times two or three trips a day. A few of the logs were so large he could take only one at a load. Some times he took two or three. Logs were not as small than as they are now. Papa built the wood part of the logging sled, bought the iron for shoes for the sled runners & other parts where needed and the neighborhood black smith helped him put them on. L. D. George did some of the iron work.

Arthur Sanders
Papa with Old Queen and Bell

Here is a picture of Papa & his logging outfit. Taken by the Woodland Store.

The logging road I spoke of before began at the South West corner of the Osborn place which is now the Lacey place, went west to the creek and turned up the canyon to the right following the creek till it reached the line between (Osborns) Laceys & our place, came on east to almost North of the Osborn (now Lacey) buildings, turned north and went in to the road about half way between the school house and the store. He went east here to the corner between Grandpa Kenworthys place & Austin George place (Where Harold Bacons old house now is). Went up to Austins barn lot crossed it between the house and barn, crossed the creek & went west along the creek till he came to the hill & over toward the old Mason place where Gene Miller lives, went to the corner & up to the gait going into the Kellum place, crossed the Kellum or Limbocker Flats to what is now called the Scott place and on to the Collins Mill located on the flat just north of the old Frank Mason house on the corner.

He finally got the lumber hauled home. He hauled sand & gravel from Pardee with the team & wagon *[Wow! Those poor horses.]* to build the chimneys and foundations for the house (not cars in those days) or trucks).

He hauled rock to fill the trenches for the foundation, that was not so bad for he used local rock around here. I don't know how long after he began the foundation that we moved into the house but it was the fall of 1911 in Nov when we moved into the house and it was by no means finished. Just the kitchen and dining room enclosed to shut out the cold. The windows were also in. The chimneys were up & we had fire. No doors to the east side, we just had carpet hung up to keep out the cold.

The rest of the house went slow but we lived in it & had lots more room & were fairly comfortable.

Mildred's Diary Extracts

[Mildred kept a diary from 1943 until June of 1974, with periodic gaps jumping years at a time. Like many country folks, much of the journal was about the day's happenings. How the garden was doing, how many quarts of fruit were canned, who came to visit, who died, etc. Reading the journal took me back to how I remember Woodland. I even remember the Woodland Women's Extension Club meetings. While living with my grandparents for a few weeks every summer, my Grandma Bacon would drag me to the ladies' meetings. What a sweet simple era.

The following are a few extracts from Mildred's diary, beginning with a special moment with her dad, Arthur Sanders. Arthur was debilitated by a stroke around 1939. Until his death in 1948 he was bedridden with sporadic lucidity. Mildred and family cared for him much of the time at home: As people were want to do in that day and age; outside of medical insurance and social safety nets.]

May 11 - 1943 - 2.30 P.M.

Papa has been the most rational this forenoon that he has been since before he took his bed. After he had his breakfast, I went into the room and he said, "Is this my room now"? I said "Yes, it has been for 4 years." He said, "Just like this?" I said, "Oh we took the door down, because it was hard to get around the bed & put that curtain up." He said, "Well it is a pretty good room."

Then after a little bit he said, "So much better than so many old people have.", with a choke in his voice.

Then in a little while I had to clean him up. And he said, "Oh I'm so sorry. I hope you girls will get pay for this it seems like I can't control. I just can't tell you how I appreciate how good you have been. You've all been good but you girls and some of the boys (I think he meant Ivan but just didn't have it quite clear) have had the worst of it." He said, "May God bless you in your families, that your children may be as good to you as you have to me."

Then he said, "There will be some money I think when everything is straightened up." said, "I think there ought to be $3,000.00 anyway or between 3 & 4 thousand dollars." Then he said brokenly, "Of course I'll want a decent burial, nothing elaborate, just good."

After a little he said, "I did think about donating $200.00 to the Cemetery Fund, but that will be alright, we just want things good & nice, not elaborate. That is what Mamma would want too I think. Respective parents should have a decent burial and the children should have what is left." He said, "There should be $3,000.00 to be for you 4." (It flashed through my mind, did he mean the baby they had expected or did he mean someone else) & I said, "Who four?" He said, "Oh I didn't say 4 children, $4,000.00. Of course there will be some expense for my burial."

Then I can't remember just how he said it but something about the lot, just like he thot he couldn't be buried by Mamma and I said, "Oh yes, there is room for 4 graves in that lot." I said, "I wish so much Mamma's grave was in the south end of our lots." He said, "Yes I did too, I don't hardly know how it came that it isn't." I thot that gave me a chance to see how he felt about moving it & I said I wondered if we should try to have it moved. He said, "Oh I don't think so now. A spot of ground doesn't make any difference."

Then he said, "There will need to be stones." I ask him what kind he liked. He said, "Just a plain stone, good not more than 4 ft high, base & all, not elaborate."

Apr 12 - 45. President Roosevelt died. Can't get anything on the radio but the report of all the goings on around Wash. D.C. The new president Harry S. Truman took oath of office. *Following page picture: Owen and Mildred lowering the flag on the last day of the Woodland Post Office, November 30, 1957.]*

May 11 - We went with Eunice and Dad *[She means "dad-in-law", Grandpa John. Eunice and Everett were two of Owen's siblings]* to take Everett to Lewiston to return to Farragut after a week at home on furlough. Eunice & I tried to to get hats. No hats they were all scarecrows. Decided to send to catalog house.

June 6 - 45. Herman came home for furlough. He goes back the 21. *[Owen's brother. You will read some about Herman's furloughs in Chapter 24.]*

June 23 - 45. Russell home last night at 12: Walked up from Kamiah after the bus came in. *[Mildred's son. Obviously serious about getting home since he walked the 12 miles from Kamiah up the grade to Woodland, much of it in the dark. Walking such distances was common at the time, however. My grandpa Harold Bacon routinely put his pack on his back and walked down into the Lolo canyon and up to Weippe on Sunday afternoons to join his logging crew for the week. Friday afternoon or Saturday morning he would grab his pack and walk back to Woodland. He never had a driver's license or a car.]*

[August 16, 45 to Sept. 1963. Big gap with no journal entries.]

Nov - 22 - 63. President Kennedy was shot today during the noon hour in Dallas, Texas. We had our first really cold spell yesterday morning. It was down to 20. Froze the tomatoes we had out here on the porch. *[Love the matter-of-factness in this entry. Kennedy was shot, but just as importantly for us—our tomatoes froze.*

❖

CHAPTER SEVENTEEN
Anna Svensson (1874-1925)

Anna Fredrika Svensson, circa 1901

[Anna was the older sister of Grandma Hulda Johnson. Eleven children were born to Carl and Sofia with Anna being the third oldest. Three of the children, Emma, Frans, and Wilhelm died during childhood.

The children grew up at Spången south of Linköping, Sweden. Spången is a little house, surrounded by fields along the Kinda Canal (every little farm or isolated home is named in Sweden). Grandpa Carl was a carpenter, but he was also the bridge watchman. A small footbridge at Spången served the farmers in the area who used the footpath to attend church. Across the canal, on a small knoll, about a half-mile to the east is Landeryds Church.

Then as now, small boats travel the Kinda Canal. A small maze of canals, rivers and lakes exist, which provide travel for many miles. When a boat approached the footbridge at Spången, the boat captain would ring a bell. Immediately dropping his carpentry tools, Grandpa Carl would run to the bridge where a series of cranks and pulleys would move the bridge, allowing the boat to pass without delay.

Times were difficult in Sweden and Carl and Sofia allowed each of their children the choice of whether to remain in Sweden or immigrate to America to seek a different future. Anna and her youngest sister Signe were the only two of the eight siblings who chose to remain in Sweden. The siblings were given the choice at an early age. Carl (or Charles as we knew him) came to America in 1888 at the age of 16; Axel (14), Alma (9) and Maria (15) came together in 1891; Grandma Hulda (16) in 1894; and Kenneth Victor (16) in 1903. All of the children coming to America adopted the surname of Carlborg. Anna and Signe, remaining in Sweden, kept the Svensson surname.

Later in life, Signe resented the loss of her siblings. How difficult it must have been for Carl, Sofia, Anna and Signe having lost the companionship of so much of their family. This was undoubtedly made even worse by the fact that neither Anna or Signe married or had any children. The American siblings sent money to the family in Sweden, but communication was unreliable. Letters often never survived the trans-Atlantic journey and thus were never delivered.

I visited Spången in 2016. Having seen old maps and photos of Spången, I was amazed to discover it looked much as it did in the late 1800s when the siblings were leaving...with the notable exception of the golf course occupying one of the neighboring fields to the south. We parked at the Landeryd church and walked the footpath down to Spången. The footpath features a few historical signs, even one which mentions Carl and Sofia Svensson raising their eleven children at the site. According to the sign, they were the first bridge tenders and lived there for about 24 years, from 1871 to 1895.

Anna Svensson

The sign also reads in part, here translated from Swedish; "On November 20, 1871, the first bridge guard, the carpenter Carl Fredrik Svensson and family, moved into Spången. As a bridge watchman, he was tasked with opening the bridge to passing ships at any time of day. He was not allowed to stay farther away than he could serve without delaying the arriving ships. When a ship came from Hjulsbro or Slattefors, the skipper gave a sound signal. The bridge guard would then have to turn the bridge aside before the ship arrived. During the night more signals could be needed to wake the guard."

As we hiked along the path, it was easy to imagine the family, with all the children running ahead, walking on a beautiful Sunday morning to church.

Anna liked photography and played musical instruments like her father. Anna suffered an episodic battle with breast cancer and eventually died at the age of 51 in 1925.

I have trouble thinking of Anna without melancholy. Having lost so many of her siblings to America, never having married nor had children, an early death suffering from cancer—these trials must have weighed heavily on her. Yet, written in Swedish on the last known picture of her (previous page) is, "This is how your old sister looks outside; old and frail but happy."

Thanks so much to Philippa Lodelius Ekman for all her assistance in translating Anna's letters as well as hosting us during our visit.]

Postcard to Charles, August 19, 1913

Linköping 19 August 1913

Heart felt congratulations on the birthday, from Father and Mother. It comes a little late, but better late than never. I will soon write a letter to you. I enjoyed the holiday but traveling today to my place. Signe is in Stjärnorp. Greetings from all of us.

Your sister Anna

From Anna to Alma, August 14, 1918

Linköping 14 August 1918

Dear Sister

I now have to deliver the sad news that our dear Pappa has left us. He passed away peacefully on August 11th, he was ill for three weeks. I'm on vacation (from work) and came home just in time to take care of him, he was in great pain and was most of the time completely without sanity.

He suffered from arteriosclerosis and a heart condition, the doctor said at once that there was no hope and it was nice that he didn't have to lay for a long time but you should know that it's empty without him. We will bury him on Saturday. We've bought a grave at the new cemetery, it is expensive these days but I feel that father should have his own grave.

Mamma will travel to Signe and be there so we can be glad that mother won't need to be alone. We plan on them living in town during the winter so they won't have to sit in the dark in the countryside during the winter.

We thank you sincerely for all the money that you've sent. I don't know if you've received the letters that we've written since it's so difficult with the mail now but I hope that you will still think of Mamma and send her something when you can. Signe only has her small salary and it doesn't go far in these times. Thanks to you helping father and mother with some money from time to time, they haven't had to suffer.

Now there will be division of the estate which I find stupid when there is not a single thing to share but it's said anyway that you have to leave a writ that you don't claim any inheritance. You can be kind to let Knut *[Victor]* and Charles know since I don't have any other address to them than Hulda's. I shall write to Hulda and Mary *[Another of the siblings, Mary (Maria) was most often called May by her brothers and sisters in America. You will see her name in other letters. May remained in Minnesota.]* but the way the mail is at the moment it's not certain that all letters arrive. And don't forget, the writ has to arrive within one year, imagine if you could come yourself, that would be fun, while mother is still alive.

Mamma and Signe send you their love.

Your sister Anna

From 1 December Mamma and Signe will be living in town, Kungsgatan 32 like before until 1 March then the address will be Minsjö skola, Västra Husby.

My address is the same as before, Hamra Sanatorium, Tumba

Aunt Tilda is pretty weak so I doubt she will live for much longer, I sometimes visit her when I'm in Stockholm. Aunt Lovis lives in Rönninge, I meet her occasionally as well. Cousin Anna Karlsson says Hello

From Anna to Hulda, July 6, 1923

July 7, 1923
Minsja Skola

Dear Sister and Brother-in-Law,

It is now so long ago that I heard anything from you, that I don't even know if this is the correct address. I will try in any case. I now have to tell you that our dear little Mother has left us. She died on the 18th of June. I came home just in time to look after her for the last few days.

She only lived for four days after I came, it happened far too quickly, but we are also glad that mother did not lay sick for a long time.

It's so empty now that mother is gone. It's the worse for Signe, who has been used to having her with her since Pappa died, 5 years ago as of next month.

I will stay with Signe as long as I live. They have closed the sanatorium where I was and even though I am not healthy I cannot yet get a new place. Luckily I have a small pension of 50 kroner a month, it's not very much to live on, but since I have gotten a room with Signe it should be fine anyways.

We buried Mother in Linkoping, in the same grave where Father is buried, and now we have ordered a stone which will be set-up on the grave, and we have friends in Linkoping who will go there with fresh flowers every week. It would be nice if you sometime came to Sweden and saw your old and lonely sisters, but that we will probably never experience.

The warmest greetings,
Anna and Signe
And our love to all your little children.
Minsja Skola
Vastra Husby
Sweden

[During our 2016 visit, we visited the grave of Carl, Sofia, Anna and Signe at the Centrala Griftegårdarna, a large cemetery in the center of Linköping. We did a bit of weed pulling and left flowers. I say "grave" because the Svenssons are all buried in the same plot.

The timing of our visit was propitious indeed. Graves are usually only rented for variable spans of years before being "recycled" (nobody we asked seemed to know what happened to the remains when they are "recycled"). Fortunately, the Svensson grave was one of the rare "Perpetual" purchases. However, after a certain period, if the cemetery loses track of relatives, the headstone is removed. A small green sign near the headstone alerted us to the imminent removal of the stone. Mona Reid (one of our distant Swedish cousins and now a dear friend) assisted me in contacting the proper authorities with the end result that Mona and I are now co-owners of the burial plot.

During the pleasant months of the year, Swedes spend time every weekend fussing over the graves of their dearly departed. Areas around the headstones are carefully manicured. Annual flowers planted and watered. Cemeteries are gardens and during our visit, we accompanied our Swedish family as they tended graves in a number of different locations. The Svensson plot appeared sad and neglected compared to the others around it.

Enclosed with Anna's last letter was the following picture. On the right is the gravestone as we visited in 2016 with the additions of Anna and Signe.]

Svensson headstone at Centrala Griftegårdarna in Linköping, Sweden

CHAPTER EIGHTEEN
Hulda Carlborg (1878-1941)

Hulda Theresa Wilhelmina Svensson, circa 1898

[As you read in the previous chapter, Grandma Hulda Johnson was born in Sweden at Spången. Upon arrival, like her other siblings, she went to her Aunt Wilhelmina Egbom's farm in Providence, Minnesota. There she met Grandpa John and before long they were raising a family on a homestead in Woodland.

A number of years ago, I asked my dad what memories he had of his Grandma Hulda. She died young at 63 when dad was about three and a half years of age. Expecting dad to say he didn't remember her, I was surprised as he described his only memory of her. He was at the ranch with his mom and dad and the family was butchering hogs. Most of the family was outside carrying on the process, but as he was the "runt" of the litter he was in the house with his Grandma Hulda. Grandma was busy trimming different cuts of meat at the table. As she looked away at one point, Dad reached up and got his hand on a knife; as young boys are want to do. She hollered, grabbed his hand and averted a nasty cut. Yell's, grabs, slaps on the butt...why do the earliest memories often involve correction? Effective correction deters future misbehavior and this made an impression on dad, just as my swats on the butt insured I didn't visit Uncle Owen without asking mom first.

Dad remembered his Grandma Hulda and Grandpa John with thick Swedish accents. Dad had to listen to his Grandpa carefully to understand all he was trying to say. Some of this "accent" is subtly evident in the following letter from Hulda written to her oldest son Owen in August of 1940. Almost exactly one year prior to her death from heart complications (died August 15, 1941). Owen was working for the Forest Service at the time and the envelope was addressed to Mr. Owen C. Johnson, c/o Powell Ranger Station, Lolo Hotsprings, Montana.

Hulda truly was a homestead wife and mother. Who lovingly attended her nine children (as attested to in a future chapter) and never stopped working. She could talk like a farmer as seen in the following letter and appreciated good yields when they came.]

From Hulda to Owen, August 16, 1940

Woodland Idaho
August 16th 1940

Dear Owen,

Friday morning, a nice morning clear and cool.

I found those pictures you wanted and will send them. Auntie Anna and Clarence came over. *[Anna Ryner, Grandpa John's sister, and her youngest child, Clarence. After they sold their homestead over the hill, 1916-1919, the Ryners moved to Spokane, Washington.]* Clarence has a car he got in the East. I think Uncle Ernest helped him to get it so now we are going to fix up your birth certificate and have her to sign it. *[Owen was born on the homestead in Woodland. His Aunt Anna must have assisted with the birth and therefore a witness for the birth certificate.]*

The boys has cut 67 acers with the combine now. Herman is going to work the summer fallow now and then they are going to start on the clover.

Jack has moved in to the woodshed at Milt George plase. Everett was home to see us. He washed dishes for a week. They work fourteen hours a day then and that gives him five day vacations so he started to walk home but rode the most of the way. It take him 12 hours between his camp and Kamiah.

We are canning corn and our tomatoes is just fine. The best we have had for years. We got 38 bushels to the acre of those oats and the wheat above the orchard 26 and the other wheat field on the other side of the hill made 25.

Had a letter from Fannie. So Fannie goes to church now and Frank to. *[Frank was Grandpa John's brother and his wife was Fannie. After their Woodland homestead, they lived in the Orofino and Teakean area.]* They have a Dunkard church over there.

Heard from Linus. Is fine and making good. Victor been here for a while. He been fixing the schoolhouse. He will be done today.

Dad and the dog is getting along fine and so all the rest.

Our best love for you,

Mother

CHAPTER NINETEEN
Kenneth Victor Carlborg (1887-1963)

Kenneth Victor Carlborg, circa 1905

[Victor, as he was known by the family, was the last of the Carlborg siblings to come to America, arriving in the spring of 1903 at the age of 16. After a few years in Minnesota, Victor came to Woodland in 1905. Victor never married and lived in the Kamiah area most of his life until his death in May of 1963.

Victor was known as the one people yelled at; his hearing having been destroyed by the loud thundering booms of cannons during his service in World War I. Having learned so much in his father's carpentry shop in Sweden, Victor was an accomplished carpenter, woodcarver, artist and model builder. In addition to Swedish and English, Victor could speak Norwegian, Danish, German, French and Spanish. He used many of these linguistic skills on the front lines during the Great War. Victor was beloved by his Johnson nieces and nephews for many reasons, as you will read later.

At the ranch; Victor in the background, cousin Irene Johnson and your editor

When his brother Charlie started the P & C tool company in Oregon around 1922, Victor was there helping set up the shop. In 1925, he spent a summer in Alaska installing machinery and building a large salmon cannery. During World War II, Victor worked to build ships in Vancouver, Washington where he was the foreman of a ship-fitters crew. If you look up "handyman" in the dictionary you will probably see a *picture of Victor...well you should anyway.*

Victor was also known as a giving man, so much so that his sister Hulda felt people took advantage of him.

The longer letter that follows paints an incredible picture of the "Welcome Home" his unit was given on their return to the States. When I first read the letter, Victor's description seemed an exaggeration. Through subsequent research on my part and viewing what pictures survive of the occasion, the magnificent procession was just as he described. This event might be the single most impressive welcome any American fighting forces have received upon their arrival on home soil.

I have a few vague memories of Victor, mainly as the really old guy who liked to sit on the periphery and watch us zany kids, as seen in the picture on the previous page. As a new grandpa with "Number One Grandson" Kyler, I was pleasantly surprised how relaxing it was to join the play. To lay on the floor and play with blocks or matchbox cars soothes the soul. Nikos Kazantzakis, the author of Zorba the Greek, said: "Time is round, and it rolls quickly." Indeed it does. The thing is, time rolls quickly whether we are enjoying it or not. I think Victor understood that perfect moments, like watching children play, need to be savored. Seek to find a perfect little moment each and every day and smile and laugh out loud. Look for it, but create it if you must.

After my grandfather Ralph's death, while living at the ranch and rummaging around in one of the dormer storage areas, I found a leather suitcase. In the suitcase, in perfect condition, was Victor's WWI wool uniform, helmet, gas mask and an honorary plaque, as if Victor had just placed them there. Maybe he had, shortly after his march in the parade in Philadelphia.]

Undated French Postcard, 1919

[The following postcard was sent to Victor's nephew Owen Johnson, with the simple address of "Mr. Owen Johnson, Woodland, Idaho." It references the 1918 Spanish Flu, which was ravaging the U.S. at the time. Worldwide the Spanish Flu killed 20 to 50 million people. More than all the soldiers and civilians killed in the war which was just ending. Another reference to this pandemic is seen in one of Alma's letters to follow. And as I write this, COVID-19 ("Coronavirus") is looming...]

K.V. Carlborg
Co K, 110 U.S. Inf.
A.S.F.

Well how are you getting along with your school. I supous the Influenza is over by this time. I am having an easy time of it here. Just taking it easy. I hope we go home before long as it get to be tiresome over here sense we lost our ocupation.

From Kenneth

Victor at the ranch with one of his handmade ship models, the Lurline

From Victor to Charlie, May 18, 1919

Camp Dix, New Jersey
May 18 1919

Dear Brother

I am i U.S.A. now *["i" in Swedish means "in"...Victor slipped into Swedish there. You will see this quite often in many of the letters that follow.]* and expect to be home before long. I think I will be sent to Fort Russell, Wyoming for discharge but I am not sure.

We had a pretty good trip across the pond, only had a couple of storms, thirteen days from Brest to Philadelphia. The day we landed was a happy day for everybody on the ship. Many people came down to see the boys land and there was many a sad face looking for some lad that never will return. There was many mothers and sweethearts that still had a hope in spite of the war department report, "Killed in Action".

State of Pennsylvania got the bigest honor roll of any state so you see they sacrificed a good deal. We whent from the boat landing to Camp Dix and got new cloths and cleaned up for the parade i Philadelphia. We whent to the city the day before the parade and we surly had a good time. We captured the town without any resistance and as far as haveing lots of funn I gess I never had as much befor. We had the liberty of the city untill seven a.m. on the 15th, when we asambeled for the last time as a division.

The parade comenced at ten a.m. and it sure was worth seeing. We march down the street in column of sections, a formation that

Victor in uniform, circa 1918

required the hole street from side to side. The bayonets were fixed and would gliter in the sun like silver.

The march was eight miles long between two human walls. The people asembled was over 2,000,000 and flags was displayed from every window. Some of the large buildings had hundreds of flags. The Liberty Bell was placed outsid of Independence Hall and wagon loads of wreaths and flowers was placed at the foot of the bell for honor of the dead, which numbered over four thousand just for this division and about three times that many wounded.

When we march past the grandstand at Independence Hall the command, eyes right, was given and every man renderd the proper salut to the bell. I will never foget this parade or anything else that I have been through in the last year.

I expect to leave Camp Dix in a couple of days. It will be a troop train made up to go to Fort Russell by that time.

I brought you a pretty good souvenir from France. It is a one pounder shell. I had the thing fixed up for a cigar lighter and it sure makes a dandy to have around the office and dresser or any other place but it is to big to carry in your pocket very handy.

If you get the time come to Woodland this summer and get it. I could send it to you but rather see you come and get then you can have a nice visit with Johnys folks and syster *[another slip into Swedish!]* Alma will most likely be there.

I have not heard from Sweden for some time but I intend to go to Sweden on a visit as soon as I can.

I got a few little things for Sister Alma and Hulda and I have alredy sent a few things to May and Grace. I got a nice pillow top for May and a silk scarf for Grace. It was some of the French fancy work and you know they are experts at those things.

Well I have not much more to write about this time so I will end my letter with lots of love from your brother.

Kenneth

CHAPTER TWENTY
Alma Carlborg (1881-1965)

Alma Carolina Carlborg, circa 1899

[What a sweetheart! Alma was another of the many I wish I could sit down and converse with over a cup of coffee. She strikes me as an empath; continually fretting over her parents and siblings. Another one of those Carlborg's who married late, she never had any children.

The youngest of the Carlborg siblings to come to America, she arrived at her aunt and uncle's farm in Minnesota at the age of nine. A reality difficult to understand. Can you imagine putting your nine-year-old daughter on a boat bound for America, while wrestling with the thought you might never see her again? While visiting Sweden in 2016, we learned that Alma's brother Charlie did visit Sweden, at least on one or two occasions. As much as she desired it, there is nothing to indicate that Alma ever did, however.]

Alma with her brother Victor

From Alma to Charlie, December 18, 1918

Portland Ore
Dec 18th 1918

Dear Brother:

Many thanks for the long looked for letter that I recieved the other day. I am glad to hear that you are well. You don't mention the Spanish Influenza, haven't you been bothered with it up there in the mountains maybe. It certainly is running lose in the cities all over the world and they say it has claimed more victims than the war itself. It is very bad here i Portland and I think we have it here in this house. Mrs Scott is sick but they won't say right out that its the Flu as they call it, but I guess I'll be carefull so I wont get it myself. If it can be avoided.

I am sending you the first letter I got from sister Anna since Father died becaus I think you will understand better what she meant about those papers that you have to send home. You did not mention in your letter weather you had done anything about it or not so I take for granted you have not. But if you have not atended to it wont you pleas do it right away, so they can get that business over with while they are in town this winter.

I do not know what to do about brother Kenneth *[Victor]*. He has not recieved any of my letters yet, at least he had not the last letter he wrot, but I hope he will go home while he is over there, he said he would like to, if they would let him.

Oh yes! He has been in the fight all right but it seems that he has been spared from being hurt. His steel helmet was dented by a bullet from a German machine gun. That was a pretty close shave I should say. But the everlasting arms of a good and mercifull God have protected him, and I hope and pray that he also puts his trust in him who alone can establish peace on earth.

[After reading the above paragraph for the first time, I retrieved Victor's helmet from my library shelf. I've always wondered about the dent, but now I saw with eyes wide. Having grazed metal with a bullet once before (the hood of my 77 Ford pickup, details I'm sure you would like to hear but would be out of place in this story) I recognized the slight scratch leading up to the dent in the helmet as completely consistent with my personal experience. What stories the old helmet could tell!

I also appreciate Alma's statement in giving credit for Victor's close call to the right source... "a good and merciful God."]

Kenneth did not mention in his letter where he was and he did not yet know what they would do if they would send them right home or what. He wrote the 17th of Nov. and I got it the 14th Dec.

Christmas is almost here and as usual we are preparing to have "julotta" *[Early morning church service on Christmas day]* and "childrens fest". We are going to decorate the church and the choir is to sing and I wish you could be along.

I am not sending you any Christmas pressent, just a greeting. I have sent 50 Kronor home to mother the last two months, so I don't feel as if I can afford to give away any pressents this year and then I know you dont care, if you dont get one.

Yes by the way, who is Gladys. Somehow I dont like exactly to have you think and talk of "sweet girls". I guess maybe I am "jelous".

I had a letter from uncle Egbom and he says he cant understand why Carl dont ever write, wont you pleas send them a Christmas letter. It would do the *[illegible word]* old souls good and not harm you any. I know its terrible to ask you to write, but let Gladys wait for a couple of letters and send one home to mother and to uncle one to May one to Hulda and one to me.

Well I must stop now. I hope you will write me soon. And pleas don't förglöm att avsäga dig något arv efter pappa der finns inte mer än mamma behöver. *[Translation: "And please don't forget to give up any inheritance. After dad there is nothing more that mom needs."]*

Lots of love from sister Alma
229 Cornell Road
Portland. Ore.

[At the time Charlie received this letter he was living in McCall, Idaho, hip-deep in co-ownership of the McCall garage with his partner, John Peterson. Long hours and days and the beginnings of forging hand tools to fix Model T's...the humble beginnings of P & C Tools.

For more information about Charlie's life and the P & C Tool Co. visit my informational website, https://pnctools.com.]

Alma and her brother Charlie

From Alma to Hulda, February 8, 1920

407 Vista Ave Portland Ore
Feb 8th. 1920

Dear Sister and everyone.   Am sure I owe you a letter.   I am ashamed of myself for not writing I just keep putting it of from day to day. But I am always thinking about you.

I dont know if I have said thank you for the Christmas pressent but if I have not I do so now. Santa was very good to me indeed. I got the surprise of my young life Christmas day. Got a letter from Carl with a checque for 50 dollars in it. I tell you it would have made me faint if I had not allready found a chair to sit on. The letter itself was a big surprise and I am sure I never expected that. It helped me pay my Dr bill so thats all done now and I am so glad. He sent mother just as much and she got it (på själva julafton) *["on Christmas Eve"]*.

I had a letter from Signe.   She has written two letters that I never recieved.   Sister Anna has been very sick, they did not expect her to live. She was at the Hospital almost all summer till late in the fall but she is back in Tumba igen *["again"]* now. She had cancer of the breast, but I don't know weather she went through an operation or not.   Signe said she guessed she had written herself by this time but its no such luck that I got it if she has. I cant see why mail has to get lost now.

Oh how I wish I could go home or that Carl would go. Mother was so happy over the letter. They had not heard anything from him for three years, so you might know they thought he had

Alma (lower left) shortly after arriving in America. Upper left, her cousin Hannah Egbom.

forgotten them. But I have never given him a chance to forget.

I wonder if you know that Kenneth and Merle have a little son. They called him Kenneth William, Billie for short. So you see sister May and Herman are Grand mother and Grand father now.

And mother is Great Grand Mother. And I well I <u>am</u> getting old.

I am on the sick list today. Stayed home and went to bed so I am sitting in bed writting. Got kind of a sudden cold this morning. And as influenza is visiting us igen *["again"...again!]* I thought it would be best to take care of myself, but I am sure I will be all right Tomorrow.

Wednesday

This letter got kind of old before it got finnished as I was not all right in the morning as I thought I would be. I stayed in bed till this morning (since sunday). Had the Dr. Monday. They are not ordinary colds now days. They come with a fever attached to them. But I saw the Dr igen *[You know this word by now!]* this morning and he said I was getting along allright but to be carefull so I guess I am allright now. I'm just kind of hanging around today. Alma

I had a letter from brother Victor the other day. He said he had rented some land but did not say who from. But I hope what ever it is he will make good. Eunice *[Johnson...who would have been 15 years old and living at the ranch with the family]* told me when she wrote that Martin *[Swensson, Grandma Hulda's first cousin, at his homestead, which is now part of the ranch.]* had been <u>blown up</u> but I did not understand if he got hurt or not. I hope he did not.

You must greet Esther Anderson and Mrs and also the rest of them that remember me *[homesteaders on the backside of the ranch, the Swedish group].* I hope Viola is all right now.

Love to yourselfs and all the <u>kiddies</u>
Sister Alma

CHAPTER TWENTY-ONE
Emma Johnson (1875-1953)

Emma Olivia Johnson, circa 1893

[Emma was a part of the Johnson family who, unlike the Carlborgs, came from Sweden as a family unit in 1882. Also accompanying their family was Grandpa Carl's brother, Lars Benjamin, with his wife and children, as well as Grandma Johanna's sister, Annika ("Anna") Johnson. Two large families and a single aunt leaving Sweden and the land they and their fathers had farmed for untold generations to seek different fortunes

in America.

The Carl Johnson family settled in the area of Monmouth, Illinois and farmed. The Lars Benjamin Johnson family stayed in the Monmouth area for a short time and then found their way west to North Dakota. Aunt Anna married Axel Falk and eventually ended up in Clark County, Washington where she is buried.

Eventually, the Johnson boys, (Grandpa John, Frank and Ernest) fanned out looking to make their own way as prosperous young farmers but found the experience difficult. John, Frank, Ernest and Anna all eventually homesteaded in the Woodland area. Ernest returned to Illinois after "proving" and selling his Idaho homestead. Betty, Emma, and Grandpa and Grandma remained in Illinois.

Emma was loving, caring, and sassy (more on that in a moment). Her loving nature is reflected in the fact that she lived with her mom and dad, our Grandpa Charles and Grandma Johanna, caring for them and running the household and farm until their deaths (Johanna in 1916 and Carl in 1924). Only after their deaths, at the age of 52, did she marry Carl Larson. Carl died a few years before her in 1951. They had no children.

The first four of the following letters were written to John and Ernest who were renting a farm near Providence, Minnesota at the time. During this period Grandpa John met Grandma Hulda, who lived in the Providence area with her aunt.

Emma consistently addresses John as "Linus", his middle name. Similarly, Carl Ernest was either "Carl" or "Ernest". Likewise, my dad was alternately known as "Kenneth" or "Wayne" depending on who was addressing him.

Emma Johnson has a distinct reputation as the origin point of the Johnson women's "sassy" gene. I'm sure her wit, sassiness and sarcasm didn't originate with her. Logic would dictate the gene was present long before Emma, but she seems to be the first to give this particular genetic twist a voice through her letters.

This gene, in the editor's opinion, like the "force" referenced repeatedly in the Star Wars films, is strong in Johnson women today. Women like Cheryl, Miranda, Baylee and Mandee, to name a few.

Being a brother, father and uncle to those endowed with this genetic "gift", I have learned through the years how to test and provoke reactions that bear witness to the continued survival of this gene (much like poking a bear with a short stick). I'm sure Emma's brothers did too. The fact these letters were saved is a testament to the fact one brother probably needed a laugh and a smile now and then. Hmmm, a way to create a smile for the day—dig out an old favorite letter, make a cup of tea, read and smile!

I would have loved to have met Emma; to have "stoked the fire" with a few well-placed words and suggestions, and watched what happened! I love her despite having never met her. She was absolutely, definitively, beyond a doubt...a blood relative.]

From Emma to John, July 18, 1898

Cameron, Ill.
July 18, 1898

Dear Brother Linus,

I thought as I have a few minuts to spare, to write you a few lines and let you know that you have got a new brother-in-law. Eugene Ryner and Anna was married last Wednesday night at the preachers house. Eugene would have it that way. Fay Ryner and I were witnesses. We did not have anybody here but his folks and John and Minnie Swanson and our own. They did not let us know in time to have very many for we only knew three days before. But we had a very nice supper for them.

We had a very good time. The only thing that made me blue was to think that you and Ernest did not know. I could not help it or I would have wrote but I was nearly hurried to death to get things in order and get the things ready for the supper.

Anna might have wrote and let you know for I suppose she knew it before she let us know but she has made up her mind she will not write to you till you have answered her letters.

They are going to live in Monmouth right across the street from Hartzells. They went to their new home the same night they was married. Oh Linus you ought to have been here and seen and heard the shiveree they had. *[Shivaree's are a thing of the past now but were part of the wedding process in our area as late as the 1960s. "Shivaree": A surprise visit to the newly married couple's home usually accompanied by a noisy, obnoxious serenade and practical jokes.*

A perfect example would be my father and mother's shivaree. After their wedding in August of 1959, they rented the house on the left just prior to the intersection of Woodland Road and Johnson Road (Erickson's live there now). The pastor of the Woodland Friends Church and his wife, Wayne and Willa Piersall just moved out of the house, perfect timing for young newlyweds looking for their first home. A week after their wedding, Uncle Dennis learned that Woodlanders were planning a shivaree, and being a good brother he tipped off the newlyweds.

The night of the event Mom and Dad hid behind an outbuilding and waited for the chaos to begin. The crowd arrived hooting and hollering and availed themselves of the "empty" house. Busying themselves with mischief, like peeling labels off canned goods, for example, they never realized their intended targets had entered the house and quietly joined the fun! The first to realize the victims were now among them was Uncle Owen. He silently acknowledged their presence, with a glance and a little wry smile, and never let on to the others they had been infiltrated. Eventually, everyone caught on and the shivaree began in earnest.]

I never heard such a noise in my life. I thought they would tear the house down. Boys and girls together, we was just eating supper when they comensed. When we was done eating we let them pass through and see the bride and get a cigar. Then they was satisfied and went home all but a few that we knew, whom we asked in to eat ice-cream and cake. I wish I could send you a peace of Wedding cake but that is hardley possible but I will save you a peace till you come home and please dont wait till it spoils for then you will not think it is very good.

Remember you promised to come Xmas. Every time I write I shall remind you of it. I am going to comence on you now and I will not let up till I see you in my arms and I will hold you so tight that I will never let you go again. You have to baby me now for I am the only single sister you have got and I am going to stay single too, for I can't see a bit of fun in getting married and have an old man to quarrel with. I mean if you get one you dont love.

Dear Linus I hope you are well and happy. We are all well but Mama. She has been sick ever sence the wedding and is not well yet, but better. I think that all of her children leaving her is what makes her so sad and lonly. I asked you to come home Xmas but I know if you could see how bad Mama looks for want of seeing you, for you are her dearest child, you would come home right away. So if you can come, for I think you can do just as well here as you can out there for I am afraid Mamma will never look happy again till you do come and I should think you would hate to make her feel so bad.

Well I have not got mutch more time to write and besides I have not got any more to write about only that we are harvesting. We have got our hay put up. The hay is very nice this year. John and Frank halped Papa put it up. We are now cutting oats. It is not mutch good. Papa say all straw and no grain hardly. Marion Stone is cutting it for us.

We are having very nice weather now. It is dry but yesterdays rain done lots of good. The corn is very late this year. Some of it has not bloomed yet and some is hardly two feet tall, that whitch was planted late. O Linus can't I write business like a man, I'd like to know.

I must close for this time for I am afraid you are tired reading. I will not feel very mutch insulted if you don't read it all for that is about all I can do.

Say has Ernest changed his adress? I got a letter from him. He had it comenced Providence. If you see him tell him to let me know for I dont like to write and him not getting it. So I will not write till I hear from either one of you but I will make up for lost time when I have found out.

Well Goodby dear Linus for this time. With fondest love to you from us all. Give our love to brother Ernest when you see him. Bettie and Peterson send you both their best regards and so does Mr. and Mrs. Ryner. Doesent that sound queer. It does to me. By.

I will send you a Sweet Pea, that is the kind of boquet Anna had and it was very pretty on her snowy dress. Anna looked very nice.

[Picture on following page: Charles & Johanna Johnson family; children left to right are John, Anna, Frank, Betty (kneeling), Emma, Ernest.]

Give Ernest one of the little red ones, I will send him some next. Mamma sends you a flower from Annas Wedding. Can you tell what kind it is. It is a plox, Celias favorite.

E.O.J

Wouldent it be nice if you and Ernest surprised us with a visit. Your Mama, Papa and old maiden sister would shout for joy. I wounder if we will have a chanse. Be a good boy and dont let some fair flower lead you astray. John Yngtve, is he around their yet. What is he doing. Is he as crazy after girls as he used to be. Did you know that Jennie Anderson and John Holmquist is married. They was merried a little before the 4 of July. Write to me soon and tell me lots of news. Tell Ernest, Maud Munson is the happy mother of a bouncing boy.

Shut for good from you loving sister, Emma Olive Johnson

Cameron, Ill.

From Emma to John & Ernest, January 17, 1900

Cameron, Jan. 17. 1900

Alskade Bröder, *["Beloved brothers"...and this repeated greeting makes me think of granddaughter Brielle. An independent little girl, who may or may not have Emma's sassy gene (too early to tell), but clearly loves her older brothers.]*

I hope you are both well. We have all been sick with the gripp *[believe this was an old word used for the flu]* but are all well now but mamma she is still vary poorly. She is not able to be up vary mutch, but I hope she will soon be her self again.

Dear brother, how are you fixt for this year that you are thinking of selling your farm. It must be vary near as hard to get along in Minn as it is in Ill. I don't hardly know how to commence this miserable letter it vary ner gives me the blues. But I have them already so I guess it would be kind a hard to get a thing you have all ready got, ain't it.

You want to know if Frank "allas stäte sten" *[Translates as "everyone's bump stone" or "everyone's stumbling stone"....was this used in the sense of he was a hindrance, a stumbling stone, or as someone continually bumped against...a hard luck case so to speak? We will never know how Emma meant this.]* is going to farm this year. Well it don't look very mutch like it for he has not got a place yet. If he don't farm I think he will sell or let you and papa take all he has got and goodness only knows that is not vary mutch. 4 horses, 2 colts and a little farming tools.

I think Papa and Frank will make a little more then the rent this year but we cant tell how mutch till the first of March when every thing will be settled up between them. Papa thinks it would be best if Ernest could come home and make an end of this business for good for he says that he dont want to uphold it any longer. Poor Papa, he has so much to think about. He needs pity but he has exhausted mine. Frank owes him some money, I dont exact know how mutch, some between 1 and 2 hundred dollars and he shall pay him first then maybe we can have some peace once more and will not hear that he has ruin himself on account of Frank and then I suppose it will have to be the next and so on till there ain't a shilling left for Frank.

Do you know what I thought when you said it was so vary easy to get land and money in Minn. I thought you would not want so vary mutch from here but could get along. Any how I wish you had never seen that horrid country for I know it is not any better than Ill or you would not want money from home all the time, when you know you have took till there is nothing more to take unless you take Frank and use him for a slave till you have got what he owes you. You want him to pay Larson's note. No sir, he shall never have anything to do with it.

I do not care to have you borrow money and then throw it on Frank to pay it. It shall not be. If you cannot pay it I dont believe Larson is in a hurry with it. Write and ask him about it that ain't to mutch. And there is another note that will fall due the first of March. 60 dollars that Papa had to borrow from John Krantz to make up the 200 hundred that Ernest borrowed before he went, and that Papa was not to have a thing to do with. What shall we do with it. Please be good and let us know right away.

Papa wants you to get him 50 bushels of oats for seed at market price if you can get it for that. If not get it any way. Do you want Papa to send the money to get it far in advance, if so alright he will send it.

Do not get angry at me or any of the rest of us because I have wrote sutch an awful letter. But if you get angry get mad at me for I am the only one to blame. I don't belive they would let me send this if they knew how I have wrote but it is not any use to beat around the bush when it means all the same.

I want to tell you if you dont want to sell your farm wait till the first of March, maybe things will turn out brighter then you think, for corn may be up to 40 cents by that time. If so Papa an Frank will make quite a bit I guess.

Well I guess I will not write any more now and I guess you think it is quite enough. Only I want to ask you to be sure and write an answer to this as soon as you get it. For Papa cannot rest till he hears what you intend to do. Don't forget any of my questions for then he will think I never asked.

Can you come home, do you think or will you be needed in Minn this year too. Or maybe you dont want to come home. I mean maybe you cant leave Hannah *[believe this reference was meant for Ernest]* for I suppose you have told her that you love her by now.

I am going to send you boys each a picture or else I am afraid you might forget what your old maid sister looks like. If you dont like her give her away to some one that does.

Hälsa til hudda så gott från mig. *[Translates to something like, "Say hello to Hudda from me", or "Give Hudda my best wishes". A rough phrase. The Providence, Minnesota census records for 1900 show John and Ernest renting a farm. Also apparently living at the farm was Hedda Anderson (age 52) and her three children who were 16, 13 and 6.]*

Kiss your sweethearts from me once or twice. And shake hands with some nice young batchlor for me.

I had a letter from Auntie Falk the other day. They are all well and happy. Julia *[Aunt Annika Falk's daughter]* said uncle was talking of coming back to Ill again. If he does he is vary foolish. Dont you think so.

Good by for this time and please, Oh please dont get angry at me for I am sad enough anyway. I cant remember when I ever was more lonesome then I am now.

Your loving sister, Emma

Burn this when you get it read. Dont forget to write right away.

[This letter is interesting on so many levels!

First, Emma mentions Hannah as a love interest. She appears to be a woman Ernest was sweet on, as will be seen in a following letter. Was this good-natured teasing by Emma or was there actually something there?

In about 2 years, Grandpa John would be married to Hulda. The 1900 census shows Hulda living in Minneapolis where, according to family stories, she eventually left a job as a bank teller to join Grandpa John in Idaho in January of 1902 when they married in Lewiston.

Maybe the Hannah mentioned in the letter was Hulda's cousin. Hulda lived with her Aunt Wilhelmina in Providence for a number of years following her arrival in America in 1894. Wilhelmina's daughter Hannah was 6 years younger than Hulda.

Also interesting are the obvious financial strains and pressure mentioned in the letter. Being a farmer was extremely difficult, even more so when you were making rent or purchase payments on your land. Obviously, John and Ernest's Minnesota farm didn't work out, or we might be Minnesotans instead of Idahoans.

Idaho was kinder and John and Hulda became embedded in the Idaho soil like their crops. Survival on a homestead was much simpler with no purchase or rent payments looming.

Emma had no problem saying how she felt about borrowing money from Papa or others. Maybe Emma's comments struck a chord. Maybe John realized the pressure of debt on the entire family, and that Minnesota would just bring more of the same. This letter was important to him for some reason, as he kept it his entire life, despite the admonishment to burn the letter after reading.

Emma would undoubtedly be horrified to know not only was the letter not burned after reading, but it has survived 120 years! Even worse, we are using it as a window into her soul! Despite her stern tones and plain language, her love for her brothers is plainly evident. Poverty might be fraying the family bond around the edges, but the fabric is holding strong. And at this moment, I can feel Emma nodding her head in approval at the words I just wrote.]

From Emma to John & Ernest, April 4, 1900

Cameron, Ill.
April 4, 1900

Mr. Linus and Ernest Johnson
Providence, Minn.

Dearest Brothers.

I hope you are both well and that Linus got there alright. I got your letter to-day Ernest. It made me vary glad to hear from you because your letters are always so bright and jolly. So you are batching. Well I hope you will like it or else I will feel sorry for you. For any thing you half-to do that you dont like is not mutch fun, I have found out in my daily duties.

Have you told Hannah that you love her yet or are you going to let another pretty little fellow get ahead of you. I wouldent if I was you. Why dont you ask her to come and keep house for you. She will make up for both cat and dog if she is anything like she looks on her picture. Don't get angry at me please.

I must tell you that I was at a surprise party last night. We gave them a beautiful lamp. It was a Marion Storrs. After we had been there for awhile we turned it into a dance and Celia and I danced till one. Then we went home and I dont know how long the rest stayed. Till morning I guess. Do you ever dance anymore.

Dear Linus I wrote to Larson right away and I got an answer to day. He says you can have the money till fall. I asked him to let you have 70, that will make it $125 in all. You did not tell me how many to ask for but if you dont want that many you can lay them by till you do. I want Ernest to get himself a suit if he wants it because I want him to look nice, because I am very proud of my brothers. I will send the mony in this letter by Regerstered Letters. I think you will get it alright and in time. I have not mist a minut in sending it to you. Aint I a blessing Linus. Ha Ha.

How did you find your girl, O.K. I hope. Did she eat the cake I sent her or was she to big to eat it. Was the flowers vary wilted when you got them to her. How long did you stay in Minneapolis? Was Ernest att [Swedish for "at"] the Depot to meet you? Was he glad to see you. I bet he was as glad to see you as we was. Sorry to mist you. You bad boys has caused me many hot tears.

Well I must close if I am going to mail this this evening. So good by. Our best and dearst love two you both.

Emma

Tell Mr. Carlburg I received his Hallo alright and send him Hallo back again and my regards also. Wish he would write and send me his picture so I will know how he looks.

[This "Mr. Carlburg" was Charlie Carlborg, Hulda's oldest brother. He was living in Providence at that time.]

Write as soon as you get this so I will know if you got the money alright. A kiss for you both. Ta Ta.

From Emma to John & Ernest, November 5, 1900

Cameron. Nov. 5, 1900

Dearest Brothers.

It has been quite a while since I recieved your ever welcome letter. I aught to have answered it long before now, but I am always behind time when it comes to writing. I believe it was borned in the family for I think we are all a little that way. I am sorry I have been pokin away att Linus for not writing to us folks att home, when I am the guilty one myself. But realy I have not got all the letters you wrote dear Linus. Besides I write just as much to you as Ernest for I write to you both and I am satisfied if you write to us not me alone. Not so mutch for my sake as for Mammas.

"Hurrah boys." Election time is near att hand and we will soon see if we will have McKinley and Prosperity or Bryan and Ruin. I suppose you will both cast your votes for President McKinley for he is the man, the only man.

[And of course McKinley was elected. He was assassinated six months into his term, Sept. 14, 1901.]

Dear brothers I wonder how you are geting along by this time. Wonder if it is cold and dissagreeable over where you are. I am sorry that old hag of a woman is not a little more civilized so you could at least live in peace. Oh if I was there wouldent I shake her up good for being so cranky. Has she been trying to make a mash on you since the time you told us about Linus. I believe it would not hurt her any if you sent her to her old man for a while.

What kind of crop did you have this year. I hope you had a great big one for I want you to get rich and get a house of your own, for Mamma and I want to come and see you. But we dont want to come as long as you live with old Hadda, for I am afraid she wold try to kick us out. And that would make me mad and I am afraid there would not be any Hadda left when I got through.

The corn crop in Ill is vary light this year. We are not going to get near as mutch this year as we did last year. But what there is is good and solid and if corn is a good price it will be all right.

Papa is going to move back to Ida Johnsons place next year. He is going to have Mrs Davidsons also. Frank has not rented any place yet, but he has a promis of one if McKinley gets elected as I hope he will be. It is John Maginnis place.

Well Ernest, poor Father Welsh is no more. He died last Thursday and was buried last Saturday morning. He died of tyfod fever. Now Simcox wont have to stay out of Scotchtown church anymore. At least he can not blame Mr. Welsh for it any more.

I must not forget to let you know that Mathilda Olson is married. She married a fellow from Nebeash by the name of Chas Swanson. But I was not at her Wedding for I was not tony enough. *["Tony" was an old word used in the late 1800s for "modern" or "fashionable". Today we would say "trendy" or "popular".]* I believe all my reading mates are married now but Hattie Peterson and myself.

And what do you think boys, Elmer and Erma Ryner are the proud parents of a fine baby girl and I tell you Ryners think there is not another baby but that because it is a girl. You know they are vary scarce in the Ryner family.

Walter is not in it any more, but he dont care. He eats and grows big and fat. He can walk by himself now and has been for quite awhile. Anna wonders if you got his picture that she sent to you a long time ago as she has not recieved any answer from either one of you. Write and let her no.

[Anna and Eugene Ryner's first child was Walter. He was born in October of 1899.]

There is another proud papa and that is Willie Olson, your old reading mate Ernest. Ever a fine boy that came to live with him. I guess I will close for this time, for it is geting late and besides I dont know of any more to tell just now. Only that I am still a widow, for Larson is still out in Wisconsin and I dont know when he will return to my gentle embrace. 'Per gentle eyes.'

I hope these few scratches will find you in the best of health and humor. We are pretty well att preasent but Mamma she is not vary well. I will close now with our best love to you both dear Linus & Ernest. Hoping and waiting to hear from you soon.

Two of Emma's brothers; Frank (left) and John

From Your ever loving sister.
Emma
P.S. Be sure to vote for McKinley and shake your fist at Bryan.
By By

To bad you could not come home this Fall Ernest. But we are satisfied when ever you come just so you come. Myrtle is still single and if she dont hold on to the Fox, he might get away, yet then she would expire I am sure. Myrtle wanted me to tell you to be sure and come home because she wants to see you. She said she knew that was all the good it would do but she wanted me to tell you any how.

We are having the finest weather you ever saw. It looks just like spring. The grass is growing so you can pretty near see it grow and the sun is as warm as it was in the summer. We have only had a few light frosts this fall.

From Emma to John & Ernest, December 18, 1900

Cameron. Dec 18, 1900

Dear Brothers

A Merry Chrismas and a Happy New Year to you.

I will write you a few lines in a hurry and let you know that we are all pretty well. Mamma has been better of late then she has been for a long time. It must be because we have got sutch beautiful weather. To day is a real sunney day, sunney and warm. If you come here you would think it was summer sure. The roads are dry and dusty. I dont hardly think we will get to go to Julotta in the sleigh this year.

Goodness just think it will soon be Xmas time and time for Old Santa Claus to make us a call. I hope he will remember you dear boys with bushels of good things. Only to think of you way out there on the prairie alone with that nasta old Hedda makes me nearly cry.

How I wish I could come and surprise you with my old maid self and get you an old time Xmas eve supper. But now when I cant I hope some good soul will do it in my place. Mamma was just saying that it will hardly be any Xmas without you boys and I am sure she is right, for that is the way I feel about it myself. But we will try to do our best. We will have a candle burning for you both and when we get our Xmas gifts, if we get any, I hope you will have received this letter and the little Xmas preasent that Mamma and I give you. Take half of it each and get yourself something. What ever you want with it.

[Knowing one is loved and remembered is an unequaled Christmas gift. Christmas season of 2018, three-year-old granddaughter Sierra was asked by her parents what she wanted for Christmas. Number one on her list was "A picture of Papa." My favorite Christmas ever.]

I hope you will be remembered by some of your friends in Minn. Do you boys intend to stay att home for your Xmas. If you do Ernie, as you are the [youngest?] make a merry Xmas for your old man Linus. I wish I was there I would make a jolly time for you both.

Do you no I became an old maid yesterday. Aint that vary sad. *[Emma's birthday was December 17, 1875, so she just turned 25.]*

If it stays nice, Bettie and Annie and their Hubbies and babys will spend Xmas with us and I expect there will be others besides.

I havent time to write any more for this evening for Frank has gone to hitch up all ready.

I hope these few lines will reach you both in the best of health and spirit.

Close for this time with thousand Loving Chrismas Greetings and good Wishes from us all to you both Dear Brothers. Your Loving Sister.

Emma

Mamma sends you a Xmas flower to remember her and ILL by. Dont forget to have a candle burning for me and Mamma.

From Emma & Family to John, October 17, 1915

[Editor's notes: Fifteen years have passed and the passage of time results in a number of changes. John, "Linus", is now in Idaho on the farm, married to Hulda Theresa Wilhelmina Carlborg, and they have seven children. Ernest has left Idaho and is now back in Illinois.]

Monmouth Ill
Oct 17. 1915

Dear sister, Brother & Children

Since it is almost two months ago, since we had the pleasure of receiving your most welcome letter, I am sure it is time I was answering it, Many, many thanks for same. It was so bright and newsy that it made us all feel good after reading it. We had worried so about Frank, since Fannie told Anna he had left her, one thought something had happened to him. It was very kind of you to let us know about him.

Ernest had a card from Fannie a while back. She said she had been in the harvest fields this summer. Her did not say a word about Frank.

I wish Frank would write to Mama, she isent feeling a bit well now. She has a severe pain or catch in her back so she can hardly move. She has felt it for several days but it is worse to night. Papa aches all over and is not feeling very good. But Ernie & T are well.

Ernest is away helping other people most of the time now, since we got most our work done. We got between 60-70 bu *[bushels]* potatoes, they are pretty nice, about 20 bu apples I think they are very good.

From Bettie

[Around the top and side of the first page, the following in different handwriting. Some discoloration is seen on page one and yellow and green discoloration on the last page, possibly from some Pansy blossoms pressed and included in the letter, as per the following.]

Pansies are for thoughts. From Momma to you and Linus.

XXXXXXXX From Mama. Please Write. Love to all

[There seems to be a page missing as page 3 seems to start in mid thought.]

I have not heard for a long while but they were all well last we heard. Ruby & Lambert goes to High school. Lambert also reads for the Minister so he is a pretty busy boy these days. He is a fine boy, wish he could have gone with when Bettie went to see you. He wanted to so very much.

And you have five little ones in school. I am sure it keeps you going getting them all ready and off every morning. Then you and baby can have a good time all by your selves all day. Bettie said she never saw anyone think so much of her baby as you did, and she thot it was one of the biggest and finest babies she ever seen. *[The sixth child would have been Kenneth at 2 1/2, but at the time of this letter writing, baby seven had arrived and was a month old, Linus.]*

We have not heard from Anna or any of hers for a long time. Hope they are all well. Greet them from us all & tell them please to write. Mama is so lonesome to hear from them & you all. & if you ever see Frank, tell him Mama is not so well and for him please to write to her. We have had several hard frosts so the trees are all yellow and some are all ready bare. And all my lovely flowers are dead. And it is so lonly and gloomy without them.

[Upside down on the top and down the side is the following:]
Our dearest & best love to you all. Mama sends special ones.

Please write at once or as soon as you can, for we love to hear from you so much. As ever your loving sister Emma. XXXXXX for the kiddies.

[Mama was not well and died less than five months after this letter was penned. As I write this the Flaming Lips song "Do You Realize??" is playing with the lyric, "Do you realize that everyone you know someday will die, and instead of saying all of your goodbyes, let them know you realize that life goes fast. It's hard to make the good things last."]

From Emma to John, October 10, 1921

[In the opening of this letter, the reader will surely note that Emma was also a master of the "puppy dog eyes" begging, shaming technique. This letter is featured on the cover of this book.]

Monmouth Ill.
Oct 10 1921

Dear brother Linus & Family,

It has been so terrible long since any of us have heard from any of you. I thought I would write again hoping some of you will answer for we wonders so much how you all are, papa was just saying today he wonderes why none of you ever write home any more. I said I did not know. So won't you please tell us why. There are so many of you, some could surely write once in a <u>great while.</u>

I hope you are all well & happy. We are pretty well but nothing to brag about. Papa is up and around most of the time but has rheumatis aches and pains and I don't know what I have got but am tired and dumpy all the time and have been for a long time. Perhaps I need a vacation as I have not had one yet in my life. But it goes somehow so we should worry, brother mine.

Ernie was home a while last evening and we talked about you then as we often do. He said he might write to you soon, but he is very busy so he just keep putting it off.

We are having Fall here now as we have had a few frosts. The last one hard enough to freeze water so the leaves are falling and my pretty flowers are mostly all dead. I think it is the sadest time off all the year when every thing dies.

Farmers have started to pick corn already but Mr. Howard that farms our land has not started yet. We have 40 acres of corn this year and it seem to be very good, all but the price. A man told us today it was 27c a bu. [*bushel*] last Saturday. That is going some is it not. A farmer has lots of chance to get rich now, have they not? I hope we can make it some way. We still have $2,000 to pay on our little farm yet, but we still have this and next year to pay it on. So I think it will go all right.

Do you remember cousin Johan and Clara in Sweden. Johan is a brother to Alfred Frans and Lotta. Well Clara is Johans wife and she is in U.S. on a visit with her children and bro and sister. The last of Sep. they were here for about a week. Clara and her daughter Bertha Blom in Chicago and we had a lovely time. While here Bertha took some pictures of Mamma's grave, one which I will send you. It is very good, almost as plain as the original. I know you will like to see it for I do so much.

Do you ever hear from Frank. Is he still in Orofino? I want to send him one too. Sent Anna one today.

Well brother dear, this is getting quite long so I better close now. Hoping to hear from you right away. Please Linus, write to your loving sister,

Emma

The folks in Galesburg are all well. They come home quite often.

Dearest love to you all from Papa, Ernie and me.

[This single page was crammed with writing along the side, etc. No room for a closing comment or closing goodbye. As a calligrapher, albeit of limited skill, I enjoy reading a letter written with a dip pen, like this one. One can see where the pen was running dry and new ink was dipped and applied. A nice Sepia ink was used with decent quality paper. In this day and age of copy paper, quality paper is not as common as it once was.]

From Emma to Eunice, June 14, 1925

Monmouth Ill.
June 14 1925

Dearest Eunice,

Many, many thanks for all you have sent us, picture, card and letter. Was very glad to get them and to know that you thot of us so far away. I have given Bettie what you sent her. They come over nearly every Sunday. They were over today but I went to church so I did not see much of them for a storm came up as I got home and they left for home. Bettie's address is 816 East Knox St., Galesburg Ill.

I had a letter from Anna not long ago saying she might come home in July if she is able to get ready. She had rheumatism so badly when she wrote.

From Fannie I havent heard for a long time. I suppose she got sore because I could not sent them the $7.00 they wanted right away. I had just written them and told them there was no money but they did not seem to understand. I hope to be able to send them some this fall as papa wanted me to.

The crops are pretty good here but nothing extra as we had a hard frost here the last of May that froze most everything, corn, garden stuff and most all the fruit. But the corn came out all right to those that left it alone, but there was a lot of farmers that planted over. Ernest left his and it is nice now again.

Glad to hear you are all well, so are we.

Enclosed is a little gift - from Ernie and myself. It is not much.

Get what you like for it.
    Will close.
    Greet all the rest from us. With lots of love from us.

    Auntie E.J.

Note Regarding Emma's Will

[While not a letter from Emma, the following needed to be included in Emma's section. The note illustrates, as do most of the previous letters you have just read, that Emma was sassy; but also loving, concerned, empathetic and giving towards her siblings.

The following was written on a 3x5 card inserted in an envelope. The author, Lambert Peterson, was the son of Emma's sister, Betty.

Shedding additional light on this note are the following facts. Grandpa John died on July 20, 1953. Emma died July 27, exactly one week after her brother. She apparently did not know her brother had just died, nor did the rest of the family in Illinois. A fact evident in this note, where Lambert writes to his Uncle John who had died over a year earlier.]

Galesburg, Illinois
Aug. 19 1954

Dear Johnie:

I enclose check in the amount of $100 in payment of the bequest left to you in Aunt Emma's Will, would you please sign and return the enclosed receipt for filing with the court.

Yours truly, Lambert

❖

CHAPTER TWENTY-TWO
Carl Ernest Johnson (1872-1958)

Carl Ernest Johnson

[Carl Ernest was known to his family as Ernest or Ernie. Much like the other side of the family, John and Hulda quickly spread the word about homesteading in Woodland. As Austin and Sarah's farm was soon bordered by their brothers, parents, uncles and cousins, so to the northwest a Swedish contingent grew. Hulda's brother, Charlie; cousins, Oscar and Martin; and John's siblings, Ernie, Frank and Anna all grabbed up

homesteads.

The Swedish group came a few years later, so instead of enjoying the flat-lands like the George clan, they were up on the ridges and northern exposures. They did enjoy one advantage; when the early crank telephones began popping up in the community (party lines, where anyone could pick up the phone and listen to their neighbors' conversations), the Swedes spoke in Swedish and left the others wondering about the conversation they were surreptitiously listening to.

Ernie homesteaded the ridge that is now part of the Johnson ranch, which we have lately been calling Ernest Ridge, where he had a modest cabin and barn. Sometime after proving up the homestead, he sold out and moved back to Illinois.

The following letter was written by Ernest after receiving word that his brother John's wife, Grandma Hulda, had suddenly passed away (at the age of 63).]

From Ernest to John, August 18, 1941

Monmouth Ill
August 18 1941

Dear brother, niece and nephews, Got your telegram over the phone, saturday morning between half past 8 and 9 o'clock with the sad news that sister Hulda had passed away.

I was awffel sorry to hear it. I was in hopes she would get well but I guess her time was up for this world and her time to go. God knows what is best for us all.

I know that you will all miss her greatly. She was a good wife and a good mother and a good woman in every way. I alwayes liked my sister Hulda and was in hopes that I would get to see her once more. I got in my car and went to Galesburg as soon as I could in the forenoon. Got there about 10 clock, to let Emma and Larson Peterson know.

Emma got nervis about it but she took it better then I thought she would. She was sorry and sends her sympathy and love to you all, in your sorry [sorrow] and loss of wife and mother. She said she is sorry she can not write to you all.

Emma and Larson are pretty well an so is the rest of the folks. I am feeling fine and in good healt.

Dear Eunice I got your letter. I am sorry I did not answer it while your mother was alive but I am putting things of. Please write me a few lines when you can. I am closing with my best message of sympathy and love to you all in the sorry and loss of your wife and mother.

Please don't take it to hard. I know how you feel.

Ernest

Bachelor Swedes at the ranch; left to right; Oscar Lindgren, Ernest Johnson, Frank Johnson, Martin Svensson, unknown (possibly Eugene Ryner)

CHAPTER TWENTY-THREE
Kenneth Johnson (1913-2001)

Kenneth William Johnson

[Of all John and Hulda's children born and raised on the ranch, Kenneth might be the most mysterious.

Leaving the farm in 1933 to join the Navy, he disappeared from family view. Having ceased all communication the family assumed he must have some position that forbade contact, something exciting and shadowy, like Naval Intelligence. The reality was less glamorous. For whatever reason, he disappeared. Consequently, the family was unable to notify him when his mother Hulda died and he was her only child absent at the funeral.

After the war, Herman was working at the Lockheed aircraft factory in California when he mistakenly received his long lost brother's paycheck. Both were working at the factory, unaware the other was there. From that point Kenneth was again part of the family, with little or no explanation that I'm aware of.

I remember Kenneth well from the annual Johnson reunions. Much like his siblings, I remember him as intelligent and soft-spoken. During those reunions, and often through letters in the mail, my mother Lorene was persistent in begging the Johnson siblings for their memoirs. Thankfully Kenneth obliged, sharing some remarkable memories that follow.

One of my favorites is his description of riding the train from Kamiah to Lewiston in 1933. As the train chugged along, he saw cousin Oscar "there by the river...working his placer mine." That would be the last time he would ever see Oscar. For some reason, my mind easily envisions that train chugging slowly down the curvy tracks along the river past Oscar as he searched for that next speck of yellow, oblivious to the passing of family on the train. And maybe Kenneth, seeing Oscar, realized his life would be forever different. If he ever returned to the farm, the familiar would be alien.]

Memories Of The Woodland Farm

February 7, 1991

My earliest memory is about indians. When I was about four or five, a group of indians (how many I can't remember) came riding down over the hill, north of the old house. One had on a feathered headdress which led me to wonder if we were going to be scalped. They talked a bit with mom, watered their horses, and rode off down the road. Jack may remember this. I believe the older kids were in school that day.

My next memory was of Uncle Victor going off to war and returning. He gave me a bullet that I still have in my box of mementoes.

Life up on the farm wasn't all that bad; everyone had a job to do. When I was six, seven, or eight my job was to keep the wood box full of wood. It was a self sufficient farm with horses, cows, pigs, chickens, some range cattle and a big garden and orchard. It seems Dad had planted some of everything. I remember at least a half dozen kinds of apples, and there were peaches, pears, plums, cherries, grapes and a couple of apricot trees; as well as berry bushes (current and gooseberry). Also there were nut trees including the following: a Chestnut or two, some Almonds, English Walnuts, Spanish Walnuts, Black Walnuts, Hickory and Hazelnut. The Almonds, English Walnuts and Chestnuts winter killed circa 1925. The Black Walnuts, Hickory and Hazelnuts are still there.

I must tell of harvesting Black Walnuts. To get to those tasty morsels was quite a chore. In the autumn many of the nuts fell off the trees but some had to be shaken off. We gathered them up and took them to where the ground was bare and hard; there we knocked the husks off with a stick then picked up the nuts, put them in a bucket with some water, and stirred it with a stick. After a few changes of water you had some pretty clean nuts, which were dried on some screen trays. By the time all that was done your hands were a nice rich brown that stayed with you for a couple of weeks. A hammer and anvil were the proper tools for cracking them. If you did it right, you got a nice piece of meat, and in the nut business where can you find such a tasty treat. All it cost was a little brown stain on your hands.

A bit more about the garden. There were a half dozen or so of rubarb plants growing just west of the spring that was the water supply. Just west of the rubarb was an aspargus patch. These gave us the first fresh things from the garden in the early spring. *[And the asparagus still comes up every spring in that location.]*

The summer was a busy time. Not only did the hay and grain have to be harvested but Mom canned an awful lot of fruits, and some vegetables, and that was a pretty big chore, considering those were the days before pressure cookers and electricity.

Much of the produce of the farm was used right there. The milk from the cows was put through a cream separator to separate the cream from the milk. The cream was saved until a sufficient quantity was available, then it was churned into butter. When there was extra cream it was sold to a creamery. Early on it was sent to a place in Kamiah. Later it had to go to Lewiston. Over time there was two cream separators. The first was a Viking and it was housed in the old smokehouse. When it was worn out it was replaced with a DeLaral that was housed in a little lean-to on the north side of the old log house.

These were hand powered centrifuges. You had to turn the crank and get them up to speed before letting the milk flow through. The milk minus the cream? Well we drank lots of it. Any extra went to the calves of the cows that produced milk in the first place. The churn to produce the butter was a wooden affair. Like a wooden bucket except it was larger on the bottom than at the top. *[Opposite page: Johnson Ranch in the 1930s.]*

It held maybe two gallons. It had a wood cover with a round hole through which went a handle, on the end of which was a "dasher", a wheel like thing.

To make butter the cream was put into the churn and the handle moved up and down rapidly to agitate the cream until the butter separated from the liquid (whey) and formed a soft mass. In a large wooden bowl and using a wood paddle, Mom would work out the remaining liquid, and there you had two or three pounds of tasty butter. I worked that handle up and down and so did the rest of the kids. Those half dozen cows that produced that milk had to be taken care of, fed and milked twice a day no matter what. But then there wasn't any television to watch, it hadn't been invented yet.

Then there were the chickens. At first the chickens just wandered about the place, nesting in the barn or any other convenient place that suited their fancy. Later, in the mid twenties, we got a bit deeper into the egg producing business. A henhouse was built east of the house among the apple trees. This was where the hens did their work.

A smaller place just east of the woodshed was built to raise the baby chickens. Most of the food for this operation was grown right on the farm. The only thing I can remember buying was oyster shells to help the hens make all those egg shells. Of course we used some of the eggs, but most went to market, a gross at a time, a cash crop during the depression.

Besides the other animals about the farm there was always a cat or two. They got a pan of milk when we milked the cows, and then they were on their own. But there was a lot of mice around that had to be taken care of.

I can recall three dogs that we had. The first one was a mean dog. He bit Ralph so badly that Doc Bryan had to take a few stitches. Dad took care of the dog, thus we had no dogs for awhile. Then one day Frank Finney [Mable George's husband] brought some grain to be rolled. He said he had something for us kids and handed down from his wagon a gunny sack, out of which tumbled a yellow pup, and that was Sport; our best friend and protector of the family.

The third dog came into our lives by way of Harry Bolander. He was a bluish colored pup, so of course his name was Bluey. Bluey came along when Sport was maybe five or six years old. They got along well and were always ready to go hunting or out to get the cows from the pasture. One day Bluey got into real trouble. He tackled a porcupine and the extraction of the quills was painful indeed. I believe it was Jack and Ralph that did the job, while I stood around trying to be helpful. Later Bluey took on and dispatched a bobcat. When I left for the navy in 1933 they were still there on the farm. Old Sport was now gray about his muzzle and a bit arthritic, but still the protector of the family.

Electronic marvels arrived upon the farm, radio that is, maybe about the mid 1920's. My first experience with radio came about thusly. There was this guy that gave a demonstration of radio at the schoolhouse and of course we had to go see this thing. At that time, as you entered the school room at the entrance under the bell, on your right was a cloak room and on the left, sort of a utility room. This made a balcony in the school room. Along the west wall was a stairway leading up to the balcony.

This guy set up his apparatus along the south wall close by the stairway. I remember setting on the stairs with Harold Bacon listening to the static, the music, and the voices coming out of this thing, undoubtedly the marvel of the ages.

This is how we got the first radio upon the farm. Some way or other we got the contract to supply wood for the school. That's where the money came from. The radio came from Sears Roebuck and was battery operated. Not a nice little nine volt job either. It required three batteries, an "A" battery, a "B" battery and a "C" battery. It was the "A" battery that was a problem. It was a six volt storage battery and that battery had to be charged, or no radio.

Owen solved that problem. He got a car generator; I think it was a Ford. He made a wooden pulley and fastened it to the flywheel of the "Elis" engine. *[I remember this Elis engine well. As a child at the ranch, I loved watching my Grandpa Ralph fire up that old one-cylinder engine and roll grain.]* With a small belt to the generator the problem was solved. When the grain was rolled, the battery got charged and there was radio. The other batteries lasted maybe six months. It had an outside antenna that stretched from a pole at the edge of the orchard to a pine tree behind the woodshed. It must have been a hundred feet long. The radio wasn't much used in the summer because of static conditions. *[The mount point for that old antenna is still in the tree behind where the old wood shed was.]*

Since I mentioned the rolling mill, I must say Pop had quite an operation going there. The grain to be rolled was delivered to the top floor of the wagon shed and put in a large hopper from which it flowed to the mill below. He not only rolled the feed for the horses, cows and pigs but also rolled feed for the neighbors. He also had a "burr" mill. This he used to grind wheat into graham flour which was used in the bread making and as a hot breakfast cereal, but that is another story.

In the bread making I remember Mom growing her own yeast. She did this in an earthen ware crock. When she made bread, which was twice a week, (nine of us kids to feed, you know) she saved some of the liquid that her yeast grew in for a starter and then fed the yeast plants with the water in which she cooked the potatoes. I remember a couple of times when the yeast died out and she borrowed a fresh start from the neighbors. The Anderson's come to mind but I'm not sure. Later she bought yeast which came in squares like cookies. Whether it improved the quality of the bread I can't say. At least it was more convenient, but the taste of a slice of warm bread fresh from the oven with butter on it was a treat I'll remember the rest of my life.

Of course Mom made such goodies as cakes, pies and cookies, but she also made what she called "dog bread". What the ingredients were was a bit of a mystery. It had a consistency a bit harder than cornbread. I'm sure it contained a lot of graham flour produced by Dad's "burr" mill. This dog bread was a part of the diet of Bluey and Sport. It must have been good; they thrived on it.

[Picture on following page: Some of the Johnson kids & friends cooling off in Lolo Creek. Left to right; Jack Johnson, Ralph Johnson, Eunice Johnson, Esther Anderson, Verna Johnson, Minnie Finney.]

Cleaning the wheat before grinding it into graham flour was done in a hand powered "fanning mill". This device removed the chaff and weed seed from the grain by passing it over a series of screens and subjecting it to a blast of air. It had an elevator that would put the grain into a sack for you, if you so wished. This mill was also used to prepare the seed grain for planting.

The seed was also treated with a copper compound to protect the crop from "smut" a fungus disease. At first this was a wet operation. A gunny sack with about a bushel of seed in it was dipped into a barrel of a solution of Blue Vitrol (copper sulfate) and then placed in a wagon box that had a tight bottom to drain away the excess fluid. The seed then was planted before it could sprout. Later this rather inconvenient treatment was replaced by using a powdered copper compound that was called "copperas" or "cuperous". Dad did a bit of engineering and came up with a method of applying it to the seed.

As I remember it, he made a square box about three feet long and eighteen inches wide. One side was fitted with a tight lid that was on hinges. The ends were fitted with pintles that fit into slotted bearings on the stand that he built for it. One end was also fitted with a hand crank. The operation of this device had to be done outdoors.

This is how it was done. A canvas was placed on the ground to catch the grain. The gadget was placed in the middle of it and about a bushel of seed was put into the box along with a spoonful of copperas. The lid closed and the crank turned about a dozen turns. When the door was opened the grain fell out onto the canvas along with a cloud of extra copperas dust that blew away with the wind, the reason for doing it outside. The grain was then scooped up and placed in sacks to be taken to the field for planting. A bit cumbersome but it got the job done.

I remember three tractors that were used upon the farm. The first was a cooperative thing with some of the neighbors. They had acquired a threshing machine and a Fordson tractor to pull it. This tractor was not big enough to do the job. It was replaced with a Lauson tractor that could handle the threshing machine.

[Following page: Woodland Road, 1929]

I don't know how it happened but Dad wound up with the whole thing. Anyway about 1929 or 1930 Dad bought the first tractor that really did the farming. It was a John Deere that not only handled the threshing job but did the plowing and eventually the rest of the farming. When the tractor took over the farming job, the horses began to disappear. Jack should have some good stories about the horses. He drove a four horse team around and around those fields.

In the good old days B.E. (Before Electricity, that is) lighting was a bit of a problem. I remember a couple of kerosene lanterns that we used about the barn and "out-of-doors". In the house there was a kerosene lamp that produced a pale yellow light just about enough to read by if you were close enough to it. Later there was a gasoline lamp that produced alot more light. Still later came an Aladdin lamp. It used kerosene and produced a good light. Those things took a bit of care cleaning the chimneys, and trimming the wicks. The gasoline job required a pump to pressurize the tank so the gas would flow. To start it a little alcohol torch was used to heat it up and vaporize the gasoline to get it started.

If I remember correctly, Linus had a bit of a problem with a bottle of gasoline for that lamp. We kept a barrel of gasoline in the wagon shed with a pump in it from which we filled a bottle with gas for use in the lamp. One evening Linus filled the bottle and replaced the cork with to much enthusiasm and the bottle shattered giving him a nasty cut in the palm of his hand that required stitches by Doc Bryan. Check that one out with Linus. *[Was Herman not Linus. Herman had the scar and told about Doc sewing it up without deadening it!]*

I must tell of the "Flexible Flyer", the coaster sled. I'm not sure, but I think Uncle Victor brought it into our lives, anyway it produced alot of winter fun for us kids. After the chores were done we would go down the hill from the wagon shed to the watering trough by the spring until it was time for supper (yup, thats the way it was, dinner at noon, supper in the evening). Later when I was in the eighth or ninth grade I took the Flexible Flyer to school and we spent our lunch hour going down the hills around the school. There was also some sledding parties. These were night time affairs, with a fire to get warm by and sometimes marshmallows to roast.

One little story about school. When I was in the tenth grade, the class had four students, Ray Hodson, Lester Craven, Paul Wood, and me. Our teacher was Miss Ora Jacks. Well one nice warm spring afternoon we played hookey and spent the afternoon exploring the Clearwater breaks. Well that didn't make any brownie points with Miss Jacks. She kept us after school until we had made up the lost time. She must have forgiven us, because on the last day of school she treated us to ice cream.

There. That's my best effort of the happenings upon the farm. I'm sure other family members can add to it.

Assorted Memories

Dear Lorene

Well its taken a year but I'll try to answer your questions as I remember it.

The buildings on the Homestead. Of course the house was there. The old barn must have been there too. It was partly log and pole construction, something the old timers would do with what was at hand. I remember Jack telling of Dad building the Shed for the Farm equipment. The grain storage and feed shed was there. I don't know who built them. But remember, at about this time, there was a sawmill just down the road. The pond is still there.

Some logging must have taken place in what became the cow pasture. I remember a pile of logs slowly decaying out there. The sawmill burned down, but rough lumber was available so probably Dad built them.

I remember building a chicken house and a small brooder house for the young chickens. Also 2 or 3 small A frame houses for mother pigs and their young. That must have been in late 1920.

Pardon the pencil, but it makes corrections much easier. On the other side is about the navy and merchant marine.

My Navy career began on March 20, 1933 in Salt Lake City, Utah as a apprentice seaman and ended March 19, 1937 as a fireman first class. The ships I served on were primarily the USS Hopkins, a World War I vintage destroyer and the USS Dobin, a tender and supply ship for the Destroyer squadron of which the

Hopkins was part of. Although my rating was fireman I actually worked in the engine room.

The Merchant Marine is different story. I can't find the book that recorded each voyage, but there is a couple of letters to the Coast Guard about upgrading my certification. So I'll do the best I can.

Before we got into the war, I'd gotten my seaman papers and had worked about a year on the SS Cathwood, a tanker owned by Union Oil Co., as a Wiper (Engine room janitor and helper) the year 1939. The war was going on in Europe.

Then came December 7, 1941, my draft board said go back to sea or become a soldier. So on September 5, 1942 I enrolled in the engineering class of the United States Maritime Service. The school was on Goverment Island at Alameda California. The course was for 90 days (and nights).

In early January 1943 I was back in Los Angeles with a third Assistant engineering certification in my hand. I was assigned to the SS Paul M. Greg a tanker owned by Union Oil Company as Third Assistant Engineer. According to the letter to the Coast Guard for an upgrade of my certificate, I was on the Greg until October 23, 1943.

The Chief Engineer of the Greg asked me to join him in taking out a new T2 Tanker, one of those that was built in Portland. So sometime in early November 1943 I became the Second Assistant Engineer of the SS Champoeg. I made two trips to the South Pacific on her and left her in New York (from a letter to the Coast Guard) on Febuary 6, 1944.

After a months vacation I was back at sea on the S.S. L.P. StClair, a Union Oil tanker as First Assistant Engineer. This was a relief from the tropics, the StClair never went further west than Hawaiian Island, north of Seattle or south of Los Angeles. In 1945 with the wars end the draft board said they didn't want me. I stayed with the StClair through its annual inspection and that was the last ship I ever boarded. The date Sept. 23 1945. I did go take the test for Chief Engineer. The date Nov. 6, 1945. I never used it.

Baseball On The Farm

A little story of baseball upon the farm. It was played west of the wood shed. The yellow rose that is still there was behind home plate and took a beating from all those wild pitches. First, second and third base were usually all in one spot, at the Corner of the old log house. The bat was a piece of an old peavey handle. The ball, a string ball and where did all that string come from? From old socks. Yup! Old socks.

Back in those days, if you was real careful you could get the top of a sock to unravel into a long string. Just what you needed to make a baseball. We had some pretty good games out there, but the yellow rose bush sure took a beating.

[Following page: Grandpa Ralph and Owen moving a load of hay, 1945.]

Letter from Kenneth

Dear Lorene,

To answer your questions I'll scratch through my rusty memory and do my best.

Yes Uncle Victor built 2 sailing ship models that I know of. The one in the picture you have must be the Lurline. That was the first one he made and was a square rigger. If I remember correctly it had 4 masts, and was much larger than the Pandora that Jerry has. The Lurline may be in the hands of Tally Fox.

There is another story about Uncle Victor that has to be told. It displays the marvelous dexterity of that man.

A way back in the 1920's Owen subscribed to a magazine called "Science and Invention." In several issues they had a contest of, "What models that could be built with matches." Yes, kitchen matches. After looking at some of the entries Uncle Victor decided he could do as well, or maybe better. So out of several boxes of matches (maybe a dozen) and a big bottle of glue he built a model of a California mission and sent it off to the magazine. I remember it being published, but I cant remember if his efforts won him a prize. But they did miss spell his name.

Some other memories of Uncle Victor. He used to come visit, usually on Sunday and always brought the Sunday paper. That was where I learned of the comic section, The Katzenjamer Kids, Tillie the Toiler and all the rest. I'm still a avid reader of the comics.

Uncle Victors hearing was badly damaged by the cannonading of World War I and ruined his musical ability which may or may not have been very good, however he brought a lot of musical instruments into our lives. I remember, a soprano saxophone, a flute, a piccolo, a clarinet (it was a metal job) and a reed organ, that I believe was Verna's. On all of these I made a lot of weird noises when I was a kid.

That brings me to your question about the Kamiah High School Band. I don't know why they ever let me into that organization, but they did. I had picked up a little skill at reading a musical score on my own and that was my musical education. It was Jack who provided the 'C" melody saxophone that I played. The time was the school years of '29-'30 and '30-31'. This was the middle of the Great Depression and there was little money for the band. The uniform was a maroon cape with a white lining. The boys wore a white shirt and white Corduroy trousers. The girls a white blouse and a white skirt. The second year a maroon beret type cap was added. For the size of the school it was a big band, 32 "musicians". Mr Harris was the conductor of my first year, Mr. Heffelfinger the second. He played a hot trumpet that disguised a lot of blue notes. In your picture I'm the guy under the Tuba on the left.

Now about Oscar Lindgren and Martin Swanson. Yes they were brothers and Mom's Cousin. Doesn't that make me a second cousin ? or something like that. The name thing goes like this. It was common practice to change your name when you came to this country in the late 1800's and early 1900's. Sence many Swedish people usually "flocked together", probably drawn by there common language and customs, they found themselves surrounded by a lot of Swanson's and Carlson's and so forth. Many took advantage of this and changed there names. Thus Oscar changed his and Martin didn't.

As I remember it, the way the name, "Carlberg" came into the family was by a brother of my mother who was the first of the family to arrive in the U.S.A. This uncle that I never knew was unfortunately killed in a harvesting accident in Minesota. He took the name Carlberg and as the other brother and sisters arrived they also took that name. *[Kenneth has Carl and Axel confused. Carl, "Charlie" was the first to come and the first to call himself a "Carlborg".*

Axel is the one who died in the threshing accident.]

In my memory there keeps poping up my mother's full name. It goes like this. Hulda Theresa Wilhelmina Swanson Carlberg Johnson. I'll bet a buck you never heard that one before, but it was around when I was a kid on the farm. If that is true then her family name in Sweden was Swanson. *[Yep, or Svensson...however you want to spell it.]*

Now back to Oscar and Martin, first Martin. As you know he had a homestead north of our place. It certainly wasn't a farm and the trees couldn't be harvested as there was no mills handy to process them. Economics was probably the reason he left for a small farm he bought near Olympia, Washington, in an area called "Chambers Prairie". I can't find it on todays map, but there was some correspondence with him at that address, as Dad looked after his interests here. Later he visited us on at least one occasion, and I remember him telling of working with a railroad mantenance crew. He married a widow (her name I don't know). She had a son that was a mining engineer, I remember him visiting us for a few days, away back when I was, maybe 12 years old. The last I knew of Martin was about 1968. *[Close. Probably 1967 since Martin died in December of that year]* Verna and Lenard stopped by my place in Federal Way one Sunday afternoon. They had come from a visit with Martin, they told me he was of frail health, I don't remember any mention of his wife, perhaps she had passed on at that time.

Oscar probably was around Woodland for some time with Martin, but I don't remember him being there. Although I knew of him and that he lived in Seattle. Later I learned that he had worked on dredges and at other water front jobs. About 1932 Oscar arrived in Woodland with a bad case of "Gold Fever". He set up a small placer operation on the Clearwater, just upstream of the old Tramway, and lived in the Pardee Cabin, which is now gone.

[Following page picture: Hulda and John Johnson and family around 1933 at the ranch.   Children left to right; Linus, Eunice, Owen, Everett, Kenneth (back), Herman, Jack and Grandpa Ralph.   Verna was probably taking the picture.]

I worked with him for a couple of months in the autumn of '32. Placer mining on the Clearwater wasn't very lucrative so I gave up when it got cold and wet in the late autumn. On my way to Boise to enlist in the Navy in March '33, as I rode by on the train, there by the river was Oscar, working his placer mine. Very much later, I believe it was Herman that told me Oscar had passed on in Seattle *[Oscar died in October of 1959]*.

My memory of Aunt Emma isn't all that good. This much I do remember. Aunt Emma and Aunt Betty came to visit us one summer, it seems that this was about 1930, and at that time I'm fairly sure that she was Mrs. Larson. That is all I can say, there is nothing more in my head.

I don't have any recent pictures of Pat or Fred. They are camera shy in there middle years. I'll have to work on that one.

Well Lorene, right or wrong thats the way I remember it, as you may have better information editors privileges are all yours.

[Or at this point, those privileges are mine. Thanks, Uncle Kenneth. Thanks for taking the time to share these wonderful "Walton-Esque" stories.]

Next summer if we can get Linus and Glenys out of Texas, and with the rest of us older guys, we may be able to come up with more and better family information for you. In the mean time this is the best I can do.

Love, O'l Uncle Ken

❖

CHAPTER TWENTY-FOUR
Herman Johnson (1917-2006)

Herman Fredrick Johnson, circa 1943

[Herman and Iris were definitely favorites of all of us.   My earliest memories of them are being at the ranch and seeing wrapped presents borne by Herman and Iris for us kids. Of course, that would make one a

favorite with any child!

Iris always had such wonderful desserts, especially the sweet, sticky Baklava she was most famous among us for. She also introduced us to the wonder of string cheese. Odd the memories we have of certain people. Iris was the first bona fide city woman we had ever met. Raised in Los Angeles, her parents owned an Armenian bakery. Always so stylish and beautiful, we often wondered what she saw in a country boy from Idaho.

Herman and Iris at the Ranch, 1960's

They came to Idaho nearly every year for a visit. Herman with a compelling desire to catch a steelhead on a yearly basis. My father enjoyed his Uncle Herman's company so he endeavored to visit with them every year when they arrived.

Herman served in WWII as a belly gunner on a B-24 bomber flying combat missions over Europe. Stationed at an airfield in Southern Italy, he flew 46 missions between July and December of 1944. On D-Day, he flew a mission bombing the beach at St Tropez, France prior to the Allied landing. He looked down on the water full of boats preparing to land the invasion, and under one newspaper photo of the same later wrote, "I looked down on this."

The family talked of him being home on leave with his hand shaking so badly he struggled to keep coffee in his cup. Crammed in a small plastic bubble, flying in an aircraft in war-time bombing raids would have done that to me as well.

They were always cheerful and when I think of them as a couple standing together, I think of their always smiling faces and the simple love obvious between them. Herman's last paragraph hints at that love and his tongue-in-cheek humor is evident as well. They married late and never had any children, but were rich with family and dearly loved by all of us.

When the family met after Grandpa John's death, the siblings decided my Grandpa Ralph would have the farm and continue the family tradition of making tender green things grow. Herman pulled Ralph aside and told him as a farmer he would be lucky to have two nickels to rub together. But he stressed the fact that Ralph should not worry about his kids, that he Herman would take care of their financial needs. And true to his word, he and Iris were very generous to Dad and his siblings. We often hear the phrase used of Herman's era, "America's greatest generation" and it certainly was...sadly it may have been our country's pinnacle.

The following summary of Herman's life is more centered on his career details and accomplishments than his upbringing. Reading almost like a list, I believe the value is in showing his personality...analytical, self-effacing, intelligent and curious. Following page photograph: Herman's log of WWII bombing missions while stationed in Italy.]

Date	Target	Place	Country	Missions
7/8/44	Markersdorf A/D (west of)	Vienna	Austria	1+2
7/9/44	Oil Refineries	Ploesti	Romania	3+4
7/13/44	Marshalling Yards	Brescia	Italy	5
7/15/44	Oil Refineries	Ploesti	Romania	6
7/20/44	Air Drome	Fredrichasen	Germany	7+8
7/21/44	Air Drome	Horshing	Austria	9
7/24/44	Harbor + Docks	Genoa	Italy	10
7/27/44	Aircraft Factory	Budapest	Hungary	11
7/30/44	Butane + Oil Refineries	Budafuzta	Hungary	12
8/10/44	Oil Refineries	Ploesti	Romania	13
8/12/44	Gun Emplacements (West of)	Toolon	France	14
8/14/44	Gun Emplacements (Near)	Genoa	Italy	15
8/15/44	Beach Gulf st Tropez Invasion	St. Tropez	France	16
8/23/44	Oil Refineries	Vienna	Austria	17+18
8/29/44	R.R. Bridge	Szeged	Hongary	19
8/30/44	R.R. Bridge	Cupirja	Yugoslavia	20
9/1/44	R.R. Bridge	Kraljevo	Yugoslavia	21
9/5/44	R.R. Bridge	Ferrara	Italy	22
9/8/44	Marshalling Yard	Nis	Yugoslavia	23
9/12/44	Aircraft Engine Works	Monich	Germany	24+25
9/20/44	Oil Refineries	Bratislavia	Czech.	26+27
9/23/44	R.R Viaduct	Avexio	Italy	28
10/10/44	Marshalling Yards	Padua	Italy	29
10/11/44	Oil Refineries	Vienna	Austria	31
10/13/44	Marshalling Yard	Banhida	Hungary	32
10/16/44	Tank Factory (near Styer)	St Valentin	Austria	33+34
11/6/44	Marshalling Yard	Sardjevo	Yogoslavia	35
11/7/44	R.R. Line	Brenner Pass	Italy	36
11/17/44	Oil Refineries	Vienna	Austria	37+38
11/20/44	R.R Bridge	Zenica	Yogoslavia	39
11/23/44	R.R. Bridge	Zenica	Yogoslavia	40
12/6/44	Marshalling Yard	Szombathly	Hungary	41
12/11/44	Oil Refinery	Moosbierbeum	Austria	42+43
12/16/44	Marshalling Yard	Hell	Austria	44
12/19/44	Marshalling Yard	Villach	Austria	45+46

Total Missions - 46
Total Sorties - - 35
Total Hours - - - 240:30

S/Sgt Herman F. Johnson 39466301 376 Bomb Group 512 Sqdn APO 681

Introduction Letter

Los Angeles, Ca.
Aug. 23, 2002

Hi You All in Idaho

Lorene you have ask me x number of times to write something about my life. Well we were cleaning a lot of old useless stuff out of drawers and closets, and I ran across this story my supervisor Mr. Hirtler, ask me to write about my past when I decided to retire from LADW. (He added the title).

Now that I read it 25 years later I can't believe I wrote it, Hope you all get something from it.

From old Uncle Herman

Roots Of Herman Johnson

On May 18 1917 in Woodland Idaho in a log house overlooking the Clearwater River Valley and the Camas Prairie was born to Hulda and John Johnson a son named Herman there 8th of 9 children. He spent his happy childhood on a 320 acre diversified farm. With Mom, Dad, 2 Sisters and 6 Brothers to keep him straight and share in all work as well as play.

As time went on the work progressed from feeding the chickens to planting, cultivating, and harvesting of the grain and hay crops as well as rounding up the range cattle. This went on 6 years after graduating from High School when in the summer of 1941, when the United States was getting quite involved in World War II, he left the farm, leaving his parents and Kid Brother to operate the farm, which by this time had progressed from horse drawn to tractors and mechanized equipment.

He hired in a Vega Airplane Co of Burbank California doing aircraft assembly work on the Vega Ventura Bomber for England and the B17 for the U.S., but in the summer of 1943 the Army thought they needed him worse than the aircraft industry. Where he served in the Air Corps Basic Training and Airplane Armorer school in Colorado, Aerial Gunnery school in Texas, back to Colorado for Aerial Gunnery Combat Training and over seas to serve a tour of Combat duty in the 512th Bomb Squadron of the 376th Bomb Groupe of the 15th Air Force in Italy as a Belly gunner and Armorment Man on a B-24 heavy bomber.

Returned to Texas and finished his military career as an Aerial Gunnery Instructor in the same school that had taught him the

Art.

In late Autumn of 1945 went back to work now for Lockheed Aircraft doing aircraft assembly work on the P-80 that companys first Jet aircraft. Tired of factory work left and went to work for American District Telegraph Co of L.A. as a trouble shooter and repairmen on Central Office burglar, holdup and fire protection equipment. After persuing this endevor from 1946 to 1952 got tired of working nights in closed buildings and dark alleys with a flashlight in one hand a tool in the other. Decided to give the Dept of Water and Power a try, by this time you probably got the idea this guy would never be satisfied at any job for very long. However this one lasted 25 1/2 Years ending in retirement today. His first taste of an electrical career started in 1938 when he wired first of all the log house where he was born, and other residents near his home when rural electrification projects came into being.

Hiring in as an assistant electrical tester with DWP on Jan 7 1952 working in the test lab, Materials and Apparatus test section. Working on many various jobs assigned to that section. Studying at home and taking any classes given by the training section that was pertinent. In November 1953 was promoted by Civil Service exam to Electrical Tester, still working in the Materials section.

In Nov. 1958 transfered to station test section of the lab and went to work as a construction tester at Scattergood Power Plant. By the end of this project he had found a job with enough future to satisfy his needs for a life time career. Due to the lack of work when this job wound down he went to the Research lab and worked on various projects as well as Oscillograph Installation testing and maintenance. But in Feb of 1960 went back to Station Test Section to help maintain and service the systems load and frequency control equipment. At this time was sent by DWP to Leads and Northrup Co. Factory service school on Load Control and Recorder Maintainance in Philadelphia, PA.

By this time Civil Service had ruled not to give the engineering assistant exam anymore, but would accept a Calif. State EIT Certificate in lieu of the exam. This closed off all avenues of advancement for a Tester, as there was no senior or principal testers at that time. A decision had to be made so he chose to give the EIT a try. First some knowledge had to be obtained, he enrolled in the evening division at L.A. City College fall semester 1961 by the finish of the fall semester of 1965, felt he had enough know how to try, but went on to take some EIT review refresher courses through Belmont High and the training section, and after his third try at the EIT in July 1967 passed and received his certificate.

In the mean time the job had gone on working as an electrical tester at Haynes Steam Plant Units 1,2,3, and then had been Y rated to Senior Electrical Tester on Unit 4.

At about this time in his career he had taken the now available Senior Electrical Testers exam and was hired as one in Jan of 1966 still working at Haynes Unit #4. This job completed and in June 1966 went to Hoover Power Plant for 4 months as Vacation and Military Leave Relief. Then back to L.A. and Unit 6 at Haynes. When the job ended he was asked to do field test engineering on construction jobs in R&D. This bent the rules a little but this straightened out when later in 1967 he earned the title when appointed to Engineering Assistant via of the EIT, and went on to work in this capacity on such projects as the 138KV to 230KV conversion at RSK, to receive the power output of Scattergood Unit #3, the conversion of several older DS stations to supervisory control; the rebuilding of the Load Dispatchers office; the check out of new DS stations and numerous small jobs in between.

Some where around June of 1968 he completed a 54 hr Power Electrical Engineering review course given by DWP training section, and in 1970 his supervisor at that time Mr. Hirtler thought he would be a good candidate for the DC Converter and Transmission System and went to the University of Wisconsin for a course on extra high voltage DC power transmission systems. However the project did not excite Herman very much and he dident spend very much time there.

In Sept. 1975 was assigned to Hoover Power Plant as the Principal Electrical Tester - as a working supervisor of the test lab facilities in the maintainance testing and repair of the control systems and instrumentation of 13 generating units and 2 house units, the coordination of test activities on joint operated equipment. Engineering revisions to existing systems as requested by Operating Dept. and kept prints current. And gave technical assistance to the operating and maintaince Depts. And performed related duties at the switch yards and McCullough Switching Station.

All of a sudden he became 60 years old and requested retirement. And that is why we are here today.

P.S. Back in 1954 Herman met Iris. A whirlwind romance went on till 1959, when they decided to try marriage, and he has been living with the same woman all these years.

End of story, July 1, 1977

Conclusion

There they exist.

In the pages they authored lie their fears, struggles, hopes and dreams; the intangible somethings that create the personality in all of us. Rising as a mist from their pages, personalities form. A turn of phrase here, a slip of the tongue there. A hidden smile peeking through. Anger barely concealed. Plain words spoken from the heart. Love.

Maybe having never heard their physical voices, or observed the peculiar way each walked, or saw how their smiles or frowns or glares changed their faces—we still sense each individual and marvel at their unique essence.

We hear their voices.

❖

I tackled this undertaking for my children and grandchildren, as a reference tome, a catalog of the voices of family members now gone. Reflecting during the process on the voice we leave behind, I leave the following for each of you, my children and grandchildren. Hear my voice speaking to each of you dear ones. Indulge me...this is what Grandpa's do...pontificate.

I am a book lover. Books have plots that twist and turn through various progressions, ultimately ending in a satisfying, ripened conclusion. Jarring, thumping denouements in some; gentle, whispered assurances that everyone lived happily ever after in others.

There are no last-minute plot twists here, however. Lives unfold, twisting and turning through life irrevocably influenced by personal decision and the grace of God. Short and tragic or lasting and sturdy, each of our lives unfurls at a unique pace and duration.

We all tend to favor the idea of a long life. We see centenarians as specially blessed by God. We think of them as products of prim and pious choices, perfect diets, regular exercise —all blended together with genetic blessings and some luck. Long life, a luminous evasive beacon we all want to reach and grasp for. Craving interminable existence, we hope and pray for another day with those we love.

Yes, personal choice used unwisely in rash and reckless decisions, inevitably shorten any life. But the quality of a life lies not in its duration. A life well lived can be fleeting and abbreviated, yet distilled and pure.

Just as many of these voices you have been hearing, I consider myself a professing Christian. I look outward and see people measuring themselves with yardsticks of good deeds, yet still believing death is the final snuffing of existence. They see death as a hard boot heel grinding the last smoke from a cigarette stub... after the last puff of smoke is quenched there is nothingness. Even believing nothing lies beyond, they still want to be remembered as a "good person". Their logic is problematic. One hundred years from now, absent written voices, we will no longer be remembered by the living, let alone considered a "good" or "bad" person. Everyone you know will be dead.

For some, their good deeds might be their last-ditch insurance policy, in case there really is a Creator. They see their lives poured onto the scale of justice and hope the good stuff on the one pan outweighs the bad stuff on the other.

This insurance is worthless; a fake, feeble grasping at vagaries. God wants more than a few good deeds and the New Testament makes it painfully clear. All our good deeds are worthless if we haven't first fallen on our knees before God and sorrowed over and repented of our bad deeds. Secondly, we are told everlasting joyful life only comes for those who believe in Christ and accept His sacrifice and punishment on behalf of us, for our bad deeds. Then the good deeds start to matter.

The happiest, brightest lights I have known were those who modeled their lives after Jesus Christ. How can a teenage Cystic Fibrosis patient live cheerfully, hopefully, purposefully? Death and suffering around the next corner, yet not living a false representation to be remembered as a "brave person", just palpable honesty from a light shining deep within. I looked at such a life and felt the supernatural presence of God within.

Do you seek a long happy life? Start with a proper foundation, Jesus Christ, and endeavor to make as many wise decisions as possible based on that foundation. Think of it as building a house. Begin with that solid foundation of Christ. Use strong beefy materials (prudent decisions). Build block by solid block, not constructing with the slippery sands. Approval of false friends, temporary pleasures with lifetime repercussions, addictions wreaking havoc, are examples of poor decisions, quicksand that might quickly destroy your "house".

Christ said, "I am the vine; you are the branches. Those who remain in me, and I in them, will produce much fruit. For apart from me you can do nothing." Apart from daily deriving sustenance from Christ, we are dead sticks.

My life has been blessed beyond measure, despite making a few, inevitable, wrong choices along the way. Falling off, I dusted off my knees and stepped back on that foundation stone. I have never regretting falling on my knees before God, acknowledging my selfishness, and asking Christ to rebuild me.

The best detail is this: No matter how screwed up our lives become, how dark the alleyway we find ourselves in, how many bad decisions compounded in layers; we can still come back to Christ. The thief dying on the cross next to Christ exercised faith, and despite a lifetime of increasingly bad choices, was told he would soon be with Christ in paradise.

I love you all...even those of you yet unformed. I have no greater desire than to see you later in heaven, with me, before Christ.

❖

Relationship Diagram: Haskins-George

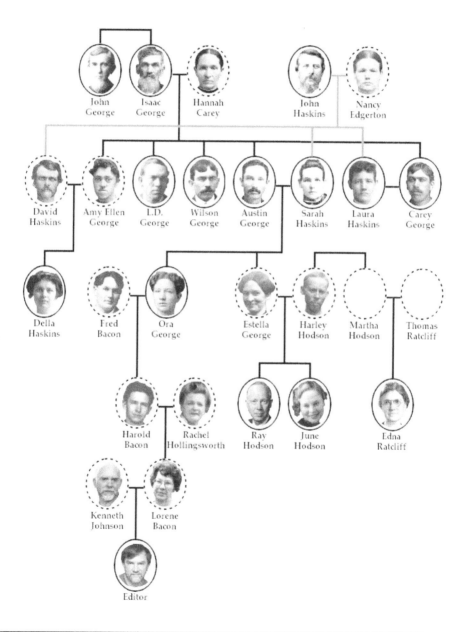

Relationship Diagram: Hollingsworth

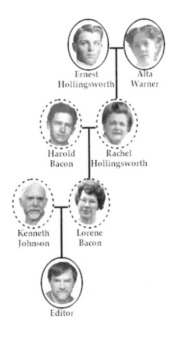

Ernest
Hollingsworth

Alta
Warner

Harold
Bacon

Rachel
Hollingsworth

Kenneth
Johnson

Lorene
Bacon

Editor

Relationship Diagram: Henderson

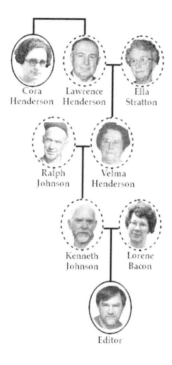

Cora
Henderson

Lawrence
Henderson

Ella
Stratton

Ralph
Johnson

Velma
Henderson

Kenneth
Johnson

Lorene
Bacon

Editor

Relationship Diagram: Johnson

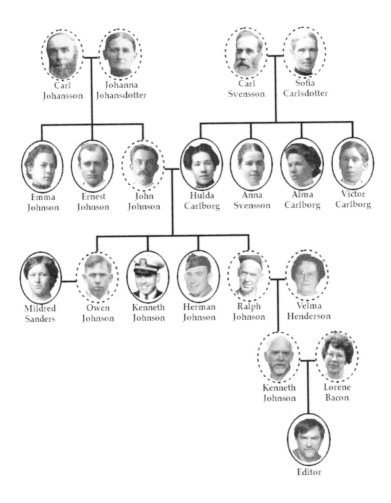

Acknowledgments

This volume exists because of the assistance of many individuals. Some of which include the following:

First and foremost, my **Lord Jesus Christ** who has blessed me far more abundantly than I deserve or expect. His grace and mercy toward me and all those willing to accept Him continue to amaze me.

Lorene Johnson, my mother, and continual inspiration. Who collected these letters, stories and pictures and has never ceased in her efforts to keep those who went before remembered.

Sandy Johnson, my wife who patiently endures my crazy larks and "next greatest ideas." Who silently smiles knowing how much work I create for myself, even when I don't.

June Hodson Schoeffler, another of the family historians on the George-Haskins side who remembered and shared. June's daughter **Donna Schoeffler Aldas Utter**, who gave so much in her books, Tales From Sarah's Shoebox and Re-tracing Sarah's Wagon Train From Kansas to Washington 150 Years Later.

Ann Warofka, Mildred Johnson's granddaughter, who graciously allowed me access to Mildred and Owen's photo albums, scrapbooks and journals.

Kathy Ackerman, my main proofreader, editor and friend, who worked hard so I would sound like an adequate, marginally acceptable writer.

❖

About the Editor

Born and raised in north-central Idaho, Jerry Johnson has been stewed in a caldron of family history and stories. Walking and enjoying the properties of his ancestors, he is continually amazed at the volume of back-breaking work coupled with grinding poverty many of the past generations triumphed in. Their stories continue to impress and inspire new generations.

A voracious reader, Johnson grew up in an environment lacking the distractions of television and internet on Red River near Elk City, Idaho. His imagination flourished.

Your editor and Raegan, who brings sunshine to every photo.

After high school graduation in 1977 in Kamiah, he went on to earn a bachelor of arts degree in Biblical Studies at Big Sky Bible College in 1981. Since that time, he has enjoyed careers in logging and law enforcement.

Never content to know enough about family and regional history, he passes time in the dark Idaho winters researching and authoring papers for his children and grandchildren. One such winter produced the website, https://pnctools.com, which chronicles the tool company built by two Swedish immigrants, one of whom was Charlie Carlborg, his great-great-uncle.

He continually thirsts for hugs and snuggles from his grandchildren. This volume is his gift to them.

"A happy family is but an earlier heaven."
George Bernard Shaw

Made in the USA
Monee, IL
29 July 2023

40044663R00193